" Everyone has
the prevention of child abuse!"

Patti Bell
and
Debbie Leonard

Through the Cracks

Through the Cracks

Horrendous Child Abuse
and Murder

Patti Alsop Bell and
Debbie Leonard

VANTAGE PRESS
New York

The authors gratefully acknowledge Mikeal Wright for permission to reprint his editorial, originally published in the *Vincennes Sun-Commercial* November 15, 1990.

FIRST EDITION

Published by Vantage Press, Inc.
516 West 34th Street, New York, New York 10001

Manufactured in the United States of America
ISBN: 0-533-11310-5

Library of Congress Catalog Card No.: 94-90655

0 9 8 7 6 5 4 3 2 1

In loving memory of Amy Shipley
and to her courageous sister, Danielle,
who experienced the system's failure to prevent
the alarming rise in occurrences of child abuse
and protect innocent children against these real horrors

Contents

Through the Cracks

Prologue: November 9, 1990

After a full week of teaching kindergarten in my hometown of Vincennes, Indiana, I was rushing through my house on November 9, 1990, trying to get ready to catch a train to Chicago so I could spend the weekend visiting my eldest son. As I gathered the luggage, my ride to the train station arrived in the driveway. The car horn blew as my telephone began ringing.

Fearful I would be late for the train, I considered closing the door without answering the phone. For reasons still unknown to me, I piled my belongings in the doorway and picked up the receiver.

"Patti, this is Carolyn," said the caller, a member of the Vincennes Community School Board. "This is not about your immediate family, but I have some heartbreaking news for you. It's about the Shipleys."

As I responded, "Did they kill Danielle?" I swallowed hard and cringed at the thought.

"No, it's the middle one. She didn't make it," Carolyn replied.

Now I began to shiver as I said, "Amy's dead! What did they do to her?"

"I don't know much detail, Patti. I just got a phone call from my daughter in Jasper and she heard that Dr. and Mrs. Shipley have been charged with murder and child abuse."

While I was talking with Carolyn, five-year-old Amy Shipley's lifeless body lay on a cold slab at the Lake County Coroner's Office in Crown Point, Indiana.

Part I
A Journey into the Past

1

Danielle Shipley's Inflicted Pain
(August 23, 1988, to March 27, 1989)

The ride to the train station with my two teacher colleagues was dominated by conversation concerning the recent telephone call I had received about little Amy Shipley's murder.

Once on board, I pushed my seat back, kicked off my shoes, and opened a new book that only a few hours ago I had anticipated reading. I could not begin to concentrate. I was holding the book and merely gazing at its pages. I looked out the train window once again to find myself only staring into space. Nothing was distracting me from questioning the horrible news of Amy Shipley's death. Why was this beautiful young child who had her entire future ahead of her gone forever? What were the details of the charges against her father, a doctor, and her stepmother, a nurse? Why wasn't this stopped when the warning signals were boldly flashing bright red almost two years ago? My thoughts raced as I took a painful journey into the past.

My first acquaintance with a member of the Shipley family was with five-year-old Danielle Nicole Shipley. She was enrolled as a student in my morning kindergarten class on August 23, 1988, at Vigo Elementary School in Vincennes, Indiana. When Danielle arrived, her brown pixie haircut framed her attractive dark eyes, which twinkled when she grinned. She displayed alertness, curiosity, and sociability. She was well dressed and appeared to be a healthy youngster. In comparison to her classmates, Danielle was a typical kindergartner.

Two weeks into the school year, all Vigo Elementary School parents were invited to attend a special evening session to meet their child's teacher. I explained the kindergarten routine and program to my large group of parents who were attending the meeting, stressing that top priority was placed on developing a happy, secure child.

At the conclusion of my talk, I saw Dr. and Mrs. Shipley looking at the morning readiness chart. I walked over and spoke to them. I knew they were Danielle's parents because I had seen Dr. Shipley come with his two smaller daughters to pick up Danielle at our morning dismissals. Mrs. Shipley started the conversation by asking why Danielle did not have a star on the chart for successfully printing her name. I answered that we had just begun school and Danielle needed more practice in letter formation to correct the reversals she made. Mrs. Shipley said Danielle had been printing her name since she was two years old. I assured her I felt confident that with Danielle's intelligence and fine motor control she would soon accomplish this task. Without further discussion, the Shipleys left the classroom.

The next time I met with Dr. and Mrs. Shipley was at a parent-teacher conference nine weeks into the school year. All six elementary schools in Vincennes had been dismissed at noon for these conferences. The kindergarten aide was working on a project at the back of my classroom when the Shipleys arrived for their scheduled appointment. I presented them with Danielle's report card. Her personal, social, and work habits showed a most satisfactory progress. I stated that her academic readiness areas would be included for evaluation at our next report.

Mrs. Shipley did all the talking for the couple during our conference. Occasionally Dr. Shipley responded in agreeing with her by nodding his head. She explained she was a pediatric nurse and had been the babysitter for the three children of Dr. Gary Shipley and his first wife, Rhonda. When Rhonda and Dr. Shipley were divorced, the children's mother moved to Indianapolis and Dr.

6

Shipley retained custody of their three daughters. She, Gloria, had been married to Dr. Shipley for six months. Dr. Shipley's other two children, three-year-old Amy and Krista, who was one, were not any trouble, Mrs. Shipley emphasized.

However, it was Danielle who presented lots of problems for them at home. Mrs. Shipley told me Danielle did not tell the truth and was very bad. I reiterated that Danielle had adjusted well to our kindergarten routine. She seemed eager to please. At times, Danielle was lacking in self-confidence and required extra reassurance that she was doing her tasks correctly. She absolutely was not a behavioral problem in the classroom. Mrs. Shipley said they disagreed; Danielle was a problem child.

Since Mrs. Shipley had provided me with some family background information indicating Danielle was experiencing difficulties at home, I suggested they might want to seek family counseling. She said they would think about it. When the Shipleys left after our forty-five-minute conference, which had been scheduled for a routine fifteen minutes, I told the kindergarten aide that I felt the Shipleys, especially the stepmother, were disappointed we were not having any problems with Danielle at school. She agreed.

Danielle continued to progress at a normal rate in kindergarten readiness activities. In mid-December, she returned to school after being absent for two days with the following note to me:

Ms. Bell,

Please excuse Danielle's absence. We have had a problem with incontinence and [are] unsure of how to deal with it. We had her seen medically to make [sure] there were no physiological problems, which there wasn't. If you have further questions, please don't hesitate to call.

Thank you.

Gloria Shipley

Immediately after reading the note, I sent it with a separate note from me to our school nurse, Loretta Perry, saying that Danielle, to my knowledge, had never been wet in school. I thought Loretta might like to call the Shipleys to see if she could offer any suggestions for them to cope with their concern. At the conclusion of my kindergarten sessions that day, I went to Loretta's office and checked with her to see if she had been able to contact the Shipleys. She said when Dr. Shipley answered the telephone, he told her to wait until he got his wife and to speak to her. Loretta explained to Mrs. Shipley my note saying that I had not seen any signs of Danielle losing control of her bladder functions. Mrs. Shipley told Loretta the problem was so bad she wanted to send Danielle to school in a diaper. Loretta replied that it would not be in the best interest of the child to put her in a diaper and that she would be notified by me if Danielle started wetting her pants in school. I routinely checked Danielle and never found her outer clothing to be damp.

For two days prior to Christmas vacation, Danielle was absent from school. That year, like many years in the past, I called all my students on either Christmas Eve or Christmas Day and wished them a Merry Christmas. When I called Danielle's residence, nobody answered. The few children I could not reach I called on New Year's Eve. Once again, I was unable to find anyone home at the Shipleys'.

Danielle did not return to school after Christmas vacation on January 3, 1989. The next day I asked Loretta to check on Danielle. Loretta spoke to Mrs. Shipley on the telephone. She was told the family had spent the holidays in Florida and that Danielle had contracted the flu when they returned to Vincennes.

The following week Danielle still was not in school. I mentioned this to our principal, Bill Ritterskamp, on January 16, and he referred Danielle's continuous absence to our school attendance officer, Donna Lawrence. She called me at home later that evening to report a home visit she had made to the Shipleys earlier in the day.

Donna began the conversation by advising them that she was there because of Danielle's lack of attendance in school since before the Christmas break. She directed questions to Danielle's father. However, the stepmother responded to all her questions instead of Dr. Shipley. He appeared to be subdued during the thirty-minute visit.

One of the problems, Mrs. Shipley explained, was that they had recently taken Danielle to Riley Hospital in Indianapolis because of bed-wetting. Riley Hospital personnel said there was nothing wrong with this child. Mrs. Shipley stated that they had put Danielle in a corner because she was bad. Danielle stayed in the corner for four days. They would not let her out of her corner until she wanted to be good. After Danielle came out of the corner, Mrs. Shipley felt they had a pretty good weekend. Dr. Shipley agreed after his wife finished her explanation. Mrs. Shipley continued talking, saying they were getting Danielle a wig to wear because she was losing some hair.

Donna did not see the children while she was at the Shipley home. As she left the residence, Dr. Shipley mentioned that they disapproved of me as Danielle's teacher and wanted a conference with the school principal.

The next evening I called the Shipley residence. Despite Donna's visit the day before, Danielle had not returned to school. When Mrs. Shipley answered, I told her I had spoken with our attendance officer about their conversation. I began talking about us working together for Danielle, as we needed to communicate for her sake. Based on what Donna had told me, I asked if they would like Danielle moved to the other kindergarten classroom, as that teacher was also fully qualified.

I heard Mrs. Shipley ask her husband if he wanted Danielle to have a different teacher. She replied, "No, we will keep you!"

I specifically asked why Danielle was experiencing hair loss. Mrs. Shipley replied that she did not know, but she was looking for a wig for Danielle. I suggested she forget the wig, as the children would not notice a few hairs were gone and the wig might be too hot. I urged her to send Danielle back to kindergarten. The next day at school I informed Mr. Ritterskamp of my conversation the night before with Mrs. Shipley.

On Friday, January 20, Danielle came back to school after an absence of five weeks. When I first saw her, I could not believe she was the same child. I was expecting to see a small hair loss; instead, there were patches missing. Danielle was thinner, had prominent circles under her eyes, and was quite pale. Before Danielle left morning kindergarten, I took her to the school's office for Mr. Ritterskamp to welcome her back and view her physical appearance.

I called the Shipley home that same evening, explaining that the children had accepted Danielle's hair loss with no difficulty, but I was troubled by the amount of hair loss and her change in appearance. I had not mentioned her missing hair to Danielle because I felt she would have an easier readjustment to school without drawing attention to this. The only reply I got from Mrs. Shipley was that Danielle was probably run-down from the flu. She reminded me that she was a nurse and was watching Danielle. I informed her that I would continue to watch Danielle also and report to them on her progress in a few days.

One week later, on Friday morning, January 27, Danielle came to school with a large abrasion on her chin than resembled a rug burn. When I asked her what had happened to her chin, she said she could not remember. My kindergartners were accustomed to having me take their picture. I had one picture left in my Polaroid camera, which I used to capture the abrasion on Danielle's chin as she worked at the puzzle center. Also, Danielle had a nickel-size bruise on her upper right arm. To reward good listening, I frequently drew a star with ink on the children's hands. I drew

Danielle's star under the bruise on her arm to let the Shipleys know I had seen it. This gave them an opportunity to mention the bruise, because I intended to speak to them about the mark on Danielle's face.

Before I left school, I showed Mr. Ritterskamp the snapshot of Danielle. We discussed the alterations in her physical appearance and the changes in her personality. The seed was planted for a possibility of child abuse. However, kindergartners receive bruises from natural causes on a daily basis. Their weight often fluctuates when they are ill with the flu. It is not unusual for them to exhibit mood changes. Even though both parents were health care professionals, I had a very uncomfortable, disturbing feeling about their treatment of Danielle. Mr. Ritterskamp recommended I document my observations and conversations.

When I called that same evening, my first question to Mrs. Shipley was: "How did Danielle receive the abrasion on her chin?"

She replied, "Danielle was allergic to the dye on the pillow at the babysitter's home. Then Gary tried to rub it off."

She did not mention the bruise on Danielle's arm. I once again expressed concern for Danielle because she was not as yet bouncing back to the way she had been when I first met her. I strongly suggested they seek counseling. Mrs. Shipley said they would consider it.

On Tuesday, January 31, I dialed the Shipley home again and, as always, Mrs. Shipley answered. I asked, "Have you and your husband decided to get family counseling?" Her reply was that they had spoken to someone at Riley Hospital about Danielle, and they did not need counseling. I asked if that person at Riley Hospital had seen Danielle. She said, "No." For the third time, I requested they make an appointment for family counseling because Danielle was not functioning as she had before Christmas.

By Friday, February 3, of that same week, I was most unhappy with Danielle's schoolwork. She was not advancing on her readiness tasks according to the capabilities I knew she had. She was withdrawing more from her peers. Her physical appearance remained unimproved. Feeling frustrated for this child and bewildered by the situation, I went to Mr. Ritterskamp's office. I expressed all my feelings of uneasiness to him. My suggestion was that a call be placed from the school to the Shipleys, informing them to make an appointment immediately for counseling or we would turn the matter over to the Knox County Welfare Department. Mr. Ritterskamp concurred. He said either he would make the call on behalf of the school or I could do it now from his office.

Since I had been conversing with Mrs. Shipley, I felt a responsibility to follow through with this. Dr. Shipley answered as soon as I dialed. Because this was my first experience in dealing with Danielle's father by himself, I was relieved to talk directly with him. My heart was palpitating because I was hopeful he would acknowledge the seriousness of Danielle's condition. I did not have to search for words, expressing worry about the bags under Danielle's eyes and her pale skin color. Her loss of weight and the patches of missing hair, as well as her withdrawal and sad expression, were noted. He was told that if they did not make an appointment today for family therapy, I would have to turn this situation over to an outside agency. He replied, "I do not understand." I repeated what I had just said. Then I told Dr. Shipley I would call back Monday for their appointment time. He said, "I will have to talk to my wife."

Mrs. Shipley reached me at home that Friday evening and said she had spoken with Mr. Ritterskamp about Danielle's hair disease and would send a pamphlet explaining its treatment to the school on Monday. This was the first time I had heard about Danielle having a hair disease. I asked her why she had not told me about this. She said she thought she had. I asked why Dr. Shipley had not told me about the hair disease earlier in the day. She responded that they had told so many people, they must have forgotten to tell me. Mrs. Shipley said she had been angry with me about my phone call to her husband, but she was not angry with me anymore. If Danielle's hair condition did not clear up, she had assured Mr. Ritterskamp they would get counseling.

The following Monday Danielle came to school. She was in attendance all week, and a pamphlet about alopecia areata was delivered to the school office by the Shipleys. When the school called Dr. Bruce Mallatt, a dermatologist in Vincennes, who Dr. Shipley said was treating this hair disease, he verified that he had seen Danielle but did not disclose the reason.

Danielle was absent from school the entire week, which was February 13 through 17. I called the Shipleys on Valentine's Day, asking for someone to come by the school to get Danielle's valentines from her classmates. Dr. Shipley came right away for them. While he was there, I asked him what was wrong with Danielle. He said she had the flu. On Friday evening, February 17, I called to see how Danielle was feeling. Mrs. Shipley said Danielle's pinkeye was better. My response was that Danielle should be past the contagious stage, and I was looking forward to seeing her on Monday in school. I made a notation of the inconsistency between Mrs. Shipley's statement that Danielle had pinkeye and Dr. Shipley's diagnosis of the flu.

When Danielle returned to school on Monday, February 20, I had not seen her for nine days. She had a mark under her right eye; it looked like someone had hit her. I brushed back what hair Danielle had left of her bangs to welcome her return with a kiss on her forehead. The bangs were sticky with hair spray. I was unaccustomed to ever noticing Danielle wearing hair spray. Under the bangs was a big bruise in the middle of her forehead. Danielle's knuckles on both hands were purple and blue, and one hand was swollen.

I said, "Danielle, I love you, but I do not like the way your hands look. You must tell me what happened to them."

"My daddy beat me on my knuckles," Danielle replied.

My worst fears had become a reality. Before I could react, Danielle released her past experiences in a flurry. She expounded on how her father made her run laps outside to the barn for punishment. She had to run up and down the stairs which made the backs of her legs hurt, she said, rubbing them as she talked. She was forced to take cold showers all of the time and sleep in the laundry room in the basement. She said this was "lots of times" and she was "afraid and cold."

I knew the time had arrived to report this suffering child to the Welfare Department. I believed there was enough evidence to prove child abuse and neglect. I quietly briefed the kindergarten aide on what I had just seen and what Danielle had told me, asking her to take Danielle to Mr. Ritterskamp.

Within a short time, Loretta entered my classroom. Mr. Ritterskamp had had her thoroughly examine Danielle. In addition to what I had been able to see on her face and hands, Loretta had discovered multiple bruises on the front of the upper thighs on both legs when Danielle removed her slacks. Mr. Ritterskamp called the Welfare Department and filed a child abuse report. He asked for a police officer to accompany the caseworker to the school. The caseworker, Beth Thais, spoke hurriedly to me, interviewed Danielle, took several pictures of her various bruises, made the decision to remove Danielle immediately from the Shipley home, and scheduled an appointment at Good Samaritan Hospital to have her examined.

Vincennes police officer John Stangle met Dr. Shipley at his car when he came to school for Danielle at dismissal time and escorted him into the principal's office to join Loretta, Mrs. Thais, and Mr. Ritterskamp. The doctor was informed of the child abuse and neglect charges reported by the school against him. He could not have Danielle. His only response was, "Can I see Danielle?" He was told he could. Dr. Shipley looked placid as he walked from the principal's office. I watched him go into the nurse's office where Danielle was sitting. He quickly spoke to her, then left.

Danielle continued to attend my class, being brought there by her foster mother. Caring about Danielle's younger sisters, Amy and Krista, who were still left in the custody of their father, a man suspected of beating their older sister, I called Danielle's caseworker two days after Danielle was placed in her foster care. When I spoke to Mrs. Thais, I asked if the sisters had been examined like Danielle at the hospital. She said she could not divulge that information, but, in her opinion, the girls were doing fine.

As I left for the weekend on Friday, March 3, eleven days after Danielle had been placed in foster care, I asked Mr. Ritterskamp to please call the Welfare Department. I thought they should know about Danielle's adjustment. From my observations, she appeared happier, was responding more readily, had a better mental attitude, and her paleness was disappearing. When her foster parent picked her up at dismissal, Danielle eagerly rushed to the car. I assumed Danielle was involved in extensive therapy. I expressed my disappointment to Mr. Ritterskamp that her therapist and caseworker had not taken the initiative to ask the school how Danielle was doing.

When I returned from the weekend on Monday, March 6, Danielle handed me the following note from her father:

Mrs. Bell:

We have an appointment in Indianapolis which we can't break. Please excuse Danielle about 10:15–10:30. We will pick her up.

Thanks.
Gary Shipley

When I showed the note to Mr. Ritterskamp, I felt certain Dr. Shipley could not have Danielle. Mr. Ritterskamp reaffirmed my belief by verbalizing, "He cannot take her." Instantly, the Welfare Department's phone number was dialed, and it was at that time that Mr. Ritterskamp was informed that Danielle had been returned to the Shipley household. I was stunned and heartsick! Nothing had been mentioned to Mr. Ritterskamp about Danielle returning home during his conversation with the Welfare Department late last Friday.

The school had no choice but to allow Dr. Shipley to take Danielle. However, he did not come early, as his note indicated, but instead arrived at our usual dismissal time. As soon as I discovered Danielle had been returned to him, I thought Dr. Shipley had no intention of picking her up early that day. His note was his way of showing me he was back in control.

I was quite aware of our Welfare Department's philosophy of keeping the family together, but I felt it was too soon for this decision to have been made. Her removal had only been for thirteen days. Assuming counseling was occurring, was Dr. Shipley cured of his abusive behavior in this short period of time? I felt the healing process for Danielle was just beginning to be put in motion. Why take a chance by possibly putting her at risk again when time should have been in everyone's favor?

Terri Grumieaux, Vigo Elementary School's social worker, was made aware of Danielle's physical abuse report to the Welfare Department by Mr. Ritterskamp. Shortly after Danielle had been put back in her home, Terri made an appointment with Mrs. Thais to discuss the situation. Terri told Mrs. Thais that our school wanted to have an open communication with the Welfare Department concerning the Shipley case.

Thursday, March 16, Terri notified the Welfare Department that Danielle was absent from school. She also called Barbara Morgan, Dr. Shipley's therapist, to let her know the school was worried about Danielle being absent. Mrs Morgan was receptive to input about Danielle and asked to be kept informed about any concerns the school had.

Danielle returned to school the following day, Friday, March 17. The kindergarten aide was taking our attendance and milk count when Danielle approached me and asked, "Why am I so bad, Mrs. Bell?"

I quickly answered, "You are not bad, Danielle."

"Then why did my daddy make me drink the bottle of liquid shampoo last night?" she inquired.

Speechless, I pulled Danielle closer to me and slipped my arm around her shoulders, patting her arm lightly as she continued talking. She said her mother would not hold her mouth and demonstrated how her father pulled open her bottom jaw, held it firmly, and poured the shampoo into her mouth. She said, "It tasted awful and made me sick."

Danielle's account of being forced to drink liquid shampoo shocked me. This was my twenty-sixth year of teaching young children and never had I heard of such an atrocious experience from any of my students. Wondering if Danielle could be harboring other punishments, I asked her. She immediately began rubbing the calves of her legs, as I had seen her do a month ago on the day she was placed in foster care. Her face denoted a strained expression when she said she had to run up and down the stairs again at home because she was so bad. She continued releasing her emotions by saying, "Daddy's beginning to pull Amy around by her hair, too."

I took Danielle to Loretta and Mr. Ritterskamp. Danielle related the exact details of drinking the liquid shampoo to them. Mr. Ritterskamp went directly to his phone and reported this second incident of child abuse to the Welfare Department. When Danielle left school that morning, it was the last time I saw her as a student in my classroom, but her painful ordeal had not ended.

As winter turned to spring, the students were dismissed at the conclusion of their school day on March 17 for vacation until March 27. When we returned to school on the Monday morning after our vacation, Mrs. Shipley called the principal's secretary, withdrawing Danielle because they were moving to Jasper, Indiana. That same day Mr. Ritterskamp asked our school social worker to find out from Danielle's therapist if the liquid shampoo incident had been discussed with Dr. Shipley during therapy. When Terri spoke to Mrs. Morgan, she realized that the therapist had been unaware of the liquid shampoo incident until Terri informed her.

I remained apprehensive about Danielle's protection. Ten days had already elapsed since Danielle had been punished by her father's use of force to make her drink liquid shampoo. What was being done to stop this and to prevent other extreme punishments that might be induced? She was no longer enrolled at our school and had relocated fifty miles away from us. Who was watching out for her? Danielle had already begun to slip through the cracks.

2

Failed Intervention
(May 4 to July 11, 1989)

As the train's wheels turned and the engine chugged, taking me closer to my Chicago destination, I continued to remember Danielle and the length of time it took for the allegations of her being abused to reach the Knox County Prosecutor's Office. While Danielle was in foster care, the Welfare Department sent a preliminary report to Vigo Elementary School as required by Indiana law. This form confirmed that the school had initiated allegations of Danielle Shipley being abused on February 20, 1989. Her father, Dr. Gary Shipley, was listed as the perpetrator. A small box was checked to indicate that the Prosecutor's Office had been notified by the Welfare Department. I was confident charges would soon be filed.

However, nothing happened! School officials anxiously waited for word from the prosecutor that action was being taken. The days that passed became a month, then two. I had no idea how Danielle was coping because our contact had been severed since the Shipleys' abrupt departure to Jasper. Finally, on May 4, I felt the opportunity was available for me to question this wait on the prosecutor's decision that had seemed like an eternity to me.

One of the first-grade teachers at my school, Barbara McGaughey, was the Knox County prosecutor's wife. We both were subpoenaed by the Welfare Department on a child custody case to testify at a hearing on May 4, because Barbara and I taught two of the children involved. As we rode home together from court, I felt compelled to discuss the Shipley situation with Barbara. Until this time I had avoided the subject, not wanting to put her in the awkward position of having to defend her husband. My mouth was dry as I gained my composure and chose my words carefully.

"Barbara, I am sorry to criticize your husband, but I don't understand why Jerry has not filed criminal charges against Dr. Shipley," I stated.

"Nothing has crossed his desk about the Shipleys," responded Barbara. "I recently asked him again about this matter. He said an Evansville newspaper writer called him for a story last February because he had heard a rumor of a doctor from Vincennes who was accused of abusing his own child. Jerry told the reporter he had never received any information from the Welfare Department about a doctor implicated in child abuse. Jerry still has heard nothing from the Welfare Department about this matter."

"I am sorry to dispute his word, but then why did I see a check mark on the Welfare Department's form indicating the prosecutor had been made aware of Danielle's abuse?" I inquired.

"Are you sure you saw that?" she asked.

I said, "Yes, I am positive."

I could tell Barbara was visibly upset by my comments. As soon as we arrived at the school's office to let our principal know we were returning to our classrooms, Barbara stepped to the telephone. When her conversation ended she said, "I called my husband and he is going to phone the Welfare Department and straighten this out by telling them to bring the Shipley file to his office today."

The next morning I saw Barbara in the hall. Quietly I asked her if the Shipley file had been received. She smiled and nodded a "yes."

I then asked, "What did he think of the pictures?"

"What pictures?" she replied.

"The pictures taken by Mrs. Thais of Danielle with all her bruises last February 20," I responded.

Barbara said, "He didn't mention any pictures."

Simultaneously I rolled my eyes, shrugged my shoulders, and tossed my head back in amazement and continued down the hall to my classroom. Later in the afternoon there was a note in my mailbox to call Jerry McGaughey. I was pleased because I was quite anxious to talk to him. As soon as my kindergartners were dismissed, I got in touch with the prosecutor.

Jerry explained, "Yesterday after my wife talked to me I called our Welfare Department. I asked where the Shipley file was that I supposedly had already seen, since Vigo School's report from them stated this by their check mark in the office's box. The man said, 'The box was not checked.' I told him it was, as the child's teacher had seen it when their report arrived at school and had been wondering why I had done nothing about this child's situation. The man replied, 'She was not supposed to talk about that report.' He was enlightened with the fact that concerned citizens were allowed to talk to the prosecutor any time they wanted. He asked me to hold and left the phone for a couple of minutes. When he returned, he said, 'She's correct. Your box was checked, but it was a mistake.' He was advised to get the Shipley file in our office speedily."

Then Jerry said, "As Barbara informed you, they complied. Yesterday was the first time I had access to this report. Then Barbara phoned me this morning about the pictures they had failed to send. Another call was placed by me to the Welfare Department and I said I wanted those pictures of Danielle Shipley *now*. Because they had equipment to have videotaped statements from Danielle, I asked for those tapes, too. I was informed that that procedure is not used by them in child abuse cases. Copies of the pictures were delivered and are in front of me on my desk. I have read the report. Could you come to my office and tell me firsthand what you know?"

"Yes, of course," was my easy response.

A meeting date and time for after school were set. When I informed my principal about our conversation, we expressed confidence that at last Danielle would be safe from future harm once the evidence was presented. I took my notebook with my documentations on the Shipleys, met with the prosecutor, and felt assured by him that he was not going to ignore Danielle Shipley's need for protection from her father.

After teaching summer school during the month of June, I took a week's vacation. While I was in Arizona, a grand jury convened to discuss the Shipley case. I did not know this was going to occur on July 11, as I did not receive a subpoena before I left. Had I known, I would have rearranged my vacation plans. Nevertheless, there was the most logical witness, the victim, and enough child protective agencies involved to present testimony.

To my disbelief, an indictment was not issued. I was enraged with the grand jury's decision to do nothing to ensure Danielle's safety after all the evidence against Dr. Shipley was presented. How could the grand jury dismiss the case after a six-year-old child told about her father beating her and making her drink liquid shampoo? In addition to Danielle's testimony, weren't they alarmed by the pictures of the numerous bruises on her body? Why didn't the testimony of our school nurse, the attendance officer, the Welfare Department's caseworker, the examining doctor from the local hospital, and the Shipleys' therapist provide enough facts in Danielle's behalf to verify the child abuse allegations to the satisfaction of the grand jury? Even though I was astonished at the outcome, I believed my questions about the grand jury's hearing would never be answered, since the report was a secret to the public, and this added to my frustrations.

I felt so helpless because my hope for Danielle's protection was shattered. The system had failed to intervene for her. This child's problem of being abused by her father was not resolved. How much deviation from the normalcy of a secure, loving household would she be able to endure? The cracks had started to expand for Danielle.

3

Danielle's Vulnerability
(November 2, 1989, to January 23, 1990)

The conductor passed through the train and announced that we were going to be delayed getting into Chicago. At that moment my arrival time was trivial. More pressing was the agonizing recollection of yet another incident of Danielle being abused after the termination of the grand jury in midsummer.

It was November 2, 1989, when Carolyn Tate called. She wanted to clue me in on a conversation she had had earlier in the day during lunch with a mutual friend of ours, Nancy Gray, who lived in Jasper. Nancy brought up the subject of "an odd bunch" who were her relatively new next-door neighbors. He was a doctor with three young children whom she had never seen outside playing. Her good friend's daughter baby-sat for them. She had explicit instructions from the parents to leave the oldest girl in her bedroom with the door taped shut as a preventive measure to stop her from "stealing food." I didn't need to ask the family's name and neither did Carolyn.

Because Carolyn was a Vincennes Community School Board member, I had filled her in on the Shipley matter shortly after Vigo Elementary School reported Danielle's first abuse. This was the same Carolyn who called before my train ride to tell me about Amy's murder. Her call about Danielle's living conditions in Jasper had been exactly one year, to the month, earlier. It appeared Carolyn was destined to contact me about pain inflicted on the Shipley children, a family she had never met.

The knowledge of this most recent harmful treatment to Danielle rekindled the fire of rage burning inside me. The underlying cause for alarm had resurfaced. I kept thinking of how confused Danielle must be. My face flushed. She was forced into isolation and hunger. My skin itched. This was a rerun of my being stymied in rescuing Danielle from her hazardous home life.

I had to talk to someone who cared. I dialed our school social worker at home.

"Terri, I am sorry to bother you. I know you don't work tomorrow, but as a favor to Danielle Shipley may I impose on you to meet me in Mr. Ritterskamp's office at 7:30 in the morning?"

"Certainly! Talk to me. What's wrong?" Terri asked.

I repeated the message Carolyn had delivered. Then, I poured out my heart to Terri. "I am beside myself with this current account of Danielle's confinement behind a taped door. What's this 'stealing food'? She probably was hungry. Both parents are participating in the abuse, which I always felt but Danielle never confirmed. The Shipleys are escalating their child abuse techniques. This could be life threatening. They might kill her, Terri!"

"I agree with your analysis. Something has to be done before Danielle becomes a statistic," Terri replied.

"Here we are fifty miles away from Danielle and powerless to shield her," I said. "Thanks a lot for taking your responsibilities to kids seriously. We need more people like you. We'll discuss this mind-blowing development in the morning."

Our meeting with Mr. Ritterskamp was all too familiar. I vented my fears for Danielle. Terri was most distressed by Dr. and Mrs. Shipley's disciplinary behavior patterns. Mr. Ritterskamp, putting the well-being of this child first, asked Terri to notify the Welfare Department. I wondered if the Welfare Department would be receptive to our report or would react unfavorably with, "Not Vigo Elementary School again about the Shipleys. How could they know anything about Danielle Shipley? She doesn't even go to school there anymore."

Regardless of any possible criticism, this would not deter the school from making necessary child abuse reports. Danielle was at risk, and an investigation was in order. Terri called Danielle's caseworker and for the third time in eight months reported suspicions of child abuse.

I called Nancy in Jasper during our Thanksgiving vacation and asked her to be on alert to the activity next door at the Shipley home. She said she already was but doubted she could know what was really going on inside that house. Nancy's friend's daughter had not baby-sat since Nancy's luncheon with Carolyn. As Nancy had mentioned to Carolyn, the Shipleys were nonsocial. Nancy never saw them.

Danielle continued to remain in my thoughts and always in my prayers. On the evening of January 23, 1990, Terri phoned to say she had a call from a reliable source who had dropped a bombshell.

"This morning Judge Theobald ruled in his court to discontinue Welfare's monitoring of Danielle Shipley."

"No!" I inquired, "Why did he do such a thing?"

"I can't begin to imagine why," Terri said.

"Mr. Ritterskamp will find out about this dismissal. I have an early parent conference tomorrow. Will you please express our concerns to him?"

"Sure will," responded Terri.

By the time I reached Mr. Ritterskamp's office, he had already talked to Judge Theobald. The judge explained that the Welfare Department had no new evidence to present. Dr. Shipley had done what was required of him in the past by the court for the return of the child. Therefore, Judge Theobald had followed the law and dismissed the Welfare Department's wardship of Danielle. Dr. Shipley was required to continue in therapy. Danielle's therapist in Jasper recommended she receive services from a psychiatric center for children in Evansville. Dr. Shipley would be admitting Danielle to live a few months at the center for her treatments.

"Mr. Ritterskamp, I am still troubled by the wardship decision. Do you honestly believe this ordeal is over for Danielle?" I said.

He asked, "Where are your documentations on the Shipleys?"

"In the safe," I answered.

"Don't get rid of them. Leave them there, Patti."

As I was exiting from his office, I uttered, "I want my notebook to collect lots of dust." This was my desire only because I still couldn't shake the gnawing sense of a catastrophe brewing.

I was receptive, however, to the news that Danielle was entering a children's psychiatric center. This would at least give her a break from her parents' abusive punishments. Would her emotional wounds finally begin to heal? Could the cracks be mended at last?

Part II
Search for the Truth

4

Investigation of Amy Shipley's Fiendish Demise (November 9 to 11, 1990)

When my son Brent met me at the Chicago train station, I talked for two hours nonstop about the abuses to Danielle, the system's capability to let her slip through the cracks, and the need to search for the truth into all the details of Amy's tragic death. Realizing Crown Point was only forty-five minutes from Chicago, I had to be certain to watch the news on television.

As the late news began, I wanted to pretend Amy's death did not really happen. Maybe there had been a mistake. Instead, the picture of Amy's precious smiling face was flashed on the screen. The announcer stated that the child's murder was under investigation and her parents, Dr. and Mrs. Gary Shipley, had been arrested. When I heard the causes of death were dehydration, malnutrition, and physical abuse, I felt the release of my tears as they flowed uncontrollably down my cheeks. The realization of this unbelievable crime had been unwillingly accepted by me.

Even though it was after midnight, I knew I had to notify the Crown Point authorities about Dr. Shipley's past history of child abuse before I could attempt to sleep. When Brent turned off his television, I dialed long-distance information. I first contacted the Crown Point Police Department. They referred me to the Lake County Sheriff's Department, who were handling the case. A dispatcher took my message for a detective to get in touch with me after the weekend because I had background information relevant to the Shipley murder case.

A day that began joyfully by teaching my forty-seven kindergarten students and anticipating a marvelous weekend visiting with Brent in Chicago was drastically brought to a tense, mournful change. I went to bed emotionally drained. My concluding thoughts as I closed my swollen, moist eyes were of when I returned home to Vincennes. What would our local newspaper uncover about this wicked crime?

As soon as I was back home again I did three things that Sunday evening after I walked in the front door of my house. First, I rapidly grabbed my newspaper and read the headline: "Doctor, Wife Jailed on Murder Charges," and then an article written by staff writer Debbie Leonard. Next, I digested the article. Then, I phoned Debbie at home.

Even though I barely knew her, I had seen Debbie when she covered our school board meetings. She appeared to be in her midtwenties and was friendly and attractive. I was familiar with her reputation for seeking the facts and continuing to do so until all her sources had been exhausted. I introduced myself on the phone by summarizing my past connections with the Shipley family; then Debbie gave me an account of her weekend.

What had started as an ordinary Friday for Debbie had turned into a frenzy of activity when one of her coworkers gave her a tip about the arrest of Dr. and Mrs. Shipley. Late in the afternoon Debbie's coworker asked if she had heard about the November 8 death of Amy Shipley and subsequent arrest of her parents.

"Not on a Friday afternoon," Debbie moaned to herself, not really knowing the amount of research this story could require. Hoping to receive information before the court building in Lake County closed, she placed a phone call to the Lake County authorities. In response, a short fax message was received from the Prosecutor's Office. The message was rather vague, lacking in details, so the search for the truth continued in an effort to give readers the most up-to-date information.

Because it was after closing hours at the Knox County Courthouse, Debbie gave Jerry McGaughey a call at his home. Since part of her daily routine at the paper was picking up arrests, accidents, and other police-related matters, she had interviewed and talked with Jerry on a number of occasions. She believed she knew this conservative prosecutor well enough to converse with him in a light-hearted manner.

"Okay, Jerry," she said. "What's this Shipley mess all about?"

Jerry stated to Debbie that Amy's death was not the first time the Shipleys had been investigated on charges relating to child abuse. Jerry told Debbie how he first became involved in 1989, when his wife, a teacher at the school that had filed the child abuse reports, told him he was being criticized by school officials for not pursuing allegations of child abuse to the oldest Shipley daughter. These allegations eventually led to a grand jury investigation, but the Shipleys were not prosecuted.

Although Jerry's interview was sketchy, off-the-record comments were given to this reporter that led her in several different directions. The more Jerry talked, the more questions cropped up in her mind. She wondered what in the world had happened in Vincennes before the Shipleys left? Why were these people not prosecuted for injuring an innocent child?

Debbie was a native of Vincennes and knew many people. A wave of suspicious thoughts hit her as she proceeded throughout the weekend to investigate the Shipleys' past in the small community of about twenty thousand people. Doctors were influential in Vincennes. Good Samaritan Hospital was one of the city's biggest employers, and most of the "movers and shakers" in the town were doctors and lawyers. Debbie was skeptical of what had happened to permit this doctor and his wife, a former nurse, to "get off the hook." Rumors buzzing around town were that Dr.

Shipley had used his professional standing to sneak through the justice system without a scratch. Although Debbie knew she would need to ask some very difficult questions of people in high places, it was her goal to get to the bottom of this disaster that had put a defenseless youngster six feet into the ground.

Not completely satisfied with the amount of data she had received, Debbie placed another call to Lake County officials and was informed of the reasons why the Shipleys had been arrested. An affidavit of probable cause said officers had been dispatched to Southlake Methodist Hospital in Merrillville early the afternoon of November 8. Upon arrival, police found what appeared to be the lifeless form of a white female child, later identified as five-year-old Amy Renee Shipley. The entire length of her body on both sides had multiple bruises and wounds. Dr. Shipley had admitted spanking Amy with his hand, a hairbrush, or a belt. Mrs. Shipley had further explained that Amy slept in the bathroom because she had tried to crawl out the window one night to get something to eat.

All of this sounded quite unbelievable to Debbie. Even though reporters are supposed to be unbiased, the story of little Amy Shipley's brutal death made it difficult for Debbie to accept that Amy's father, a man who had taken an oath to help heal the sick, would have deliberately killed his child.

As Debbie continued to work, she heard the newspaper's fax phone ringing. Playing a hunch, she left her desk to see if it was for her. Without a request, the Indiana Attorney General's office had automatically assimilated more facts concerning Dr. Shipley.

In 1989, Dr. Shipley had been reviewed by the Drug Enforcement Administration for writing prescriptions for family members. He was required to give monthly reports of his prescriptions to the Attorney General's Office, see a psychiatrist weekly for codependency, and perform community service. He had to study the effects of substance abuse and appear monthly before the Medical Licensing Board. His employer, Good Samaritan Hospital in Vincennes, also was expected to report to the board, and Dr. Shipley was to notify the board if he moved from the area.

The drug problem at the Shipley house continued even after the 1989 investigations. An Indiana State Police examination in early 1990 showed that only 8 percent of the drugs Dr. Shipley had ordered could be documented for patient use during time periods reviewed by investigators. These state officers began their inquiry after a pharmacist at Memorial Hospital in Jasper began questioning the number of drugs Dr. Shipley was ordering from there. He had also purchased large quantities of drugs from the pharmacies in the Jasper area.

Dr. Shipley was placed on twenty years' probation in August of 1990 by the Indiana Medical Licensing Board. This was after a suspension four months earlier for writing prescriptions for family members during 1989.

The family moved at least five times between the time of the drug investigation and Amy's death. Welfare authorities lost track of them, but the Indiana Medical Licensing Board knew exactly where the Shipley family was located. Even though this state board of his colleagues knew where Dr. Shipley called home, it did not have the slightest idea that Dr. and Mrs. Shipley were running from one area to another to conceal child abuse allegations.

As a result of Dr. Shipley's arrest, his medical license was suspended by the Indiana Medical Licensing Board for the second time in eight months. This board's opinion found Dr. Shipley to be a clear and immediate danger to the public health and safety.

After reading the information provided by the Indiana Attorney General's Office, Debbie decided to make one more phone call before starting to write her story. She was worried about the welfare of Dr. Shipley's other two daughters, Danielle and Krista. Lake County police assured her both living children were safe. They had been placed in the custody of the Lake County Welfare Department and were in foster care.

The phone conversation presented new questions for Debbie. Why were the two sisters not with their mother, Rhonda Shipley, who lived in Indianapolis? And would Lake County welfare workers give these children the care and protection they needed?

On a notepad, Debbie rapidly condensed the pertinent data she had collected in less than twenty-four hours. She wrote:

Dr. Gary Shipley,

1. Child abuse allegations—oldest daughter, Danielle.
2. Grand jury; no prosecution.
3. DEA investigation.
4. Medical license suspended.
5. 20 years' probation by Indiana Medical Licensing Board.
6. Child abuse and murder charges—middle daughter, Amy.
7. Second suspension of medical license.

This reads like a nightmare, but it is reality!

5

Tragedy's Aftermath
(November 12, 1990, to August 5, 1991)

When Debbie returned to work after the weekend, she was curious to find out more about this upper-class professional couple accused of such heinous crimes as child neglect and murder. She began prying further into the history of the Shipley family.

Dr. Gary Shipley's earlier years seemed to be that of a fairy tale and provided no clues to what eventually happened to him and his family. He grew up in the small town of Clayton, Indiana, located west of Indianapolis. His father, Alex, was a financial analyst and his mother, Beulah, a mathematics teacher. At the time of the murder, his older brother, Frank, was a surgeon in North Dakota and his sister was a nurse in Indianapolis.

Gary played quarterback on the football team at Cascade High School, which had an eight-win season his senior year. He was a guard on the varsity basketball squad and set a school record in track. Regardless of his involvement in all these sports, he still maintained a high grade-point average in his studies. Teachers and coaches remembered him as shy and someone who did not use drugs. His track coach spoke of him as operating "cooly."

In a yearbook picture Gary was found dancing with his childhood sweetheart, Rhonda R. Hanlon. She was from nearby Coatesville, the daughter of Hope and Robert Hanlon. The couple met in the seventh grade and were members of the National Honor Society and the symphonic band. The romance continued after high school when both attended Indiana University. They were married in 1977, and in three years Rhonda graduated with an education degree. Gary graduated a year later, and the couple moved to Indianapolis for him to begin studying at Indiana University's School of Medicine. Intense higher education required money, so the couple borrowed heavily from banks and Rhonda's parents. Rhonda also worked as a junior high school teacher for remedial and problem children and took a second job to make ends meet. Rhonda began to gain weight and within a few years was described as thickset. In 1989, she began a medically supervised diet.

About the same time, Gloria Pfleiderer, a nurse from Danville, Illinois, whom Gary met at the IU School of Medicine, moved into the Shipley home as their housekeeper. After Gary completed his residency, the Shipley family relocated to Vincennes, in June 1987, and Gloria took another job. Shortly thereafter, Gloria again moved in with the Shipley family. Gary and Rhonda were soon separated. The divorce settlement stated that Rhonda abandoned her family and voluntarily committed herself to the Mental Health Pavilion of Community Hospital North in Indianapolis for treatment of depression. Gary was granted legal custody of their three preschool daughters. The divorce became final in January 1988, and three months later Gary and Gloria were married in Danville, Illinois. Rhonda apparently remained friendly with the newly married couple and was occasionally seen in their company. She also received visitation rights with her children but kept her emotional distance.

Gary's life continued to become more complicated than it had been when he was married to Rhonda. He had incurred a debt of more than $190,000. Gloria had been fired from her job at an Indianapolis hospital in 1985 due to substance abuse problems. She underwent treatment that same year, but in 1988 her nursing license was suspended indefinitely when the state nursing board determined she had relapsed. Dr. Shipley was working as a cardiovascular surgeon at Good Samaritan Hospital in Vincennes and was employed in a private practice with three other physicians. During this time, Danielle began kindergarten at Vigo Elementary School, Debbie learned, and in February and March of 1989 Danielle came to school with indications she had been physically abused and each time Vigo school officials reported Dr. Shipley, who was suspected of abusing her. In early April 1989, the Shipleys moved to Jasper and a grand jury finally convened in July at Vincennes, with the result of no prosecution of Dr. Shipley. A third report of Danielle possibly being abused while the family lived in Jasper was given to the Knox County Welfare Department. The wardship of the Welfare Department was removed in late January 1990 by Superior Court judge Edward Theobald. Dr. Shipley admitted Danielle into a child's psychiatric center at Evansville, Indiana, in March 1990, and the family moved to northern Indiana in September 1990.

Administrators at the Hammond Clinic in Munster, Indiana, might have thought they had snared quite a worker in October 1990 when they hired Dr. Gary Shipley. Being a cardiovascular surgeon, Dr. Shipley should have been able to go anywhere and easily secure employment. But, because of a shaky résumé, with four jobs in the previous three years, he had to practically beg for the job. The Hammond Clinic overlooked his recent scrapes with the Medical Licensing Board, since heart surgeons capable of earning more than five hundred thousand dollars a year didn't often end up in Munster, making less than their potential salary.

After eleven days on the job, Dr. Shipley resigned his position to accept another at Jennings Community Hospital, in North Vernon, Indiana. Shortly after his resignation, he was working one of his final shifts in the Hammond Clinic emergency room when he received a frantic telephone call from his wife to return home because of a medical emergency.

When he arrived at his home, in the well-to-do community of Lakes of the Four Seasons, he saw a parked ambulance. He found paramedics inside his home trying to revive his lifeless middle child. The sight of the girl's body shocked the medical workers, even in crime-hardened Lake County.

The citizens of Knox County were unaccustomed to dealing with child abuse to this extreme. They were stunned and alarmed after reading Debbie's first account of Amy's death. Letters to the editor of the *Sun-Commercial* were frequent. Questions were being asked as to why this child abuse with Danielle wasn't stopped in Knox County.

Sun-Commercial managing editor Mikeal Wright wrote the following in an editorial dated November 15, 1990:

> The news last weekend of the death of a former Vincennes child evokes a reaction of outrage. That this most unthinkable, unspeakable, and disgusting scenario could happen in a civilized society is appalling.
>
> In addition to examining "the system" for ways to improve it, a full investigation should be undertaken by the appropriate authorities to find answers to the myriad of questions in this case.
>
> For example, why was the older girl allowed back in the home? Why were the other children not removed from the home when abuse was alleged and cause for an investigation found? Why did it take so long for the welfare report to reach the prosecutor? Why was the older girl not allowed to testify before a grand jury investigating her case? Why was this not followed up adequately and then allowed to fall by the wayside by the family merely pulling up stakes and moving to a different part of the state? And, ultimately, how did the system allow an innocent five-year-old girl to die?

After assimilating background facts, Debbie sought answers to the same questions of what happened or did not happen with the allegations of Danielle Shipley's child abuse. Debbie approached her boss with the idea of acquiring the 1989 Knox County Grand Jury transcripts. They discussed the prospect of petitioning the court with the hopes that the release of these secretive documents would add more pieces to this incomprehensible puzzle.

In December 1990, the *Sun-Commercial* and its attorney, Ed Cummings, appeared before the judge who had presided over the Knox County Grand Jury. In the beginning, the outlook was bleak for the paper, but Mr. Cummings argued that the paper had a First Amendment right to information which is considered of paramount public importance. The *Sun-Commercial* had been flooded with calls and letters from upset citizens who believed the allegations of Dr. Shipley's child abuse had been disregarded because he was a doctor. The public wanted to know how he could have slipped through Knox County without being prosecuted. Lake County Superior Court judge James Letsinger didn't want the transcripts released to the public until after a jury had been seated because he feared that would make it impossible to find impartial jurors. After all the arguments were heard, the grand jury judge took the matter under advisement. Within a few days, the judge denied the *Sun-Commercial* access to the transcripts. He did give the paper's attorney fifteen days to submit arguments detailing how the court could release the information without breaking laws surrounding grand jury secrecy. This was promptly submitted and the Knox County community waited for a final ruling.

With the approach of Christmas, the untimely death of Amy Shipley was not forgotten by the people of Knox County. One example of this was a letter to the editor of the *Sun-Commercial* dated December 23, 1990, from George E. Lane of Bruceville, Indiana:

> In two days it will be Christmas, a time when most of us think of family and friends and send our good will to all men. It is a time of year when we look at the faces of children, happy and anxious to see what presents are under the tree.
>
> It is a time to celebrate, again, the birth of the Christ child. I will enjoy watching my own, my only, granddaughter, five-year-old Lauren Biggs, as she hurries to open her presents. As I think

of Lauren, I cannot help but think of little five-year-old Amy Shipley who lost her life at such a young age November 8, 1990.

In a press report of the *Sun-Commercial* it is reported that Amy was allegedly beaten on a daily basis by her parents and she was made to sleep in the bathroom as punishment for stealing food. The official cause of death for this young child was dehydration, malnutrition and physical abuse, the Lake County prosecutor's office reported. Hundreds of Knox County citizens feel that her brutal death would have never happened, had those who are responsible for the protection of our children from gross child abuse and neglect gone that extra mile, here in Knox County.

Hundreds of citizens who didn't know this darling little child have signed petitions asking for an independent investigation leading up to her death. Yes, seven-year-old Danielle and her sister, three-year-old Krista, have been cheated out of the growing up with Amy. The grandparents have been cheated of the joy of watching Amy open presents that she would have had. Somehow we all feel cheated by the needless death of this young child.

As we all gather with our families this Christmas, let us pause to say a prayer for this little angel who is now in the tender arms of the God of us all.

While the public was mourning this child's death, I felt at times as though I was operating in a semicoma. I was unaccustomed to talking to the news media, but there were justified requests for me to do so. Newspaper reporters and television stations for national news were frequently contacting Vigo Elementary School.

My principal and I gave our first interview to Debbie for our local southern Indiana paper five days after Amy died. Bill Dolan from the *Gary Post-Tribune* arrived at our school a few days later seeking firsthand information for his paper in northern Indiana. Geraldo Rivera's office called Mr. Ritterskamp, asking the two of us to be on his show, which we declined. *People* magazine and *A Current Affair* called me more than once at home. We eventually granted *A Current Affair* a television interview.

The Lake County Police Department had returned the phone call I made the day after Amy's death and informed me that their agency would be contacting me again. Before Christmas, I was teaching when Mr. Ritterskamp called me into his office to meet deputy prosecutors Sue Collins and Lillian Oliver and detective Tom Decanter from Lake County. They asked me specific questions about Danielle's abuse and said my principal, our school nurse, the attendance officer, and I would be on their witness list from the Vincennes Community School System.

In February, Loretta, Donna, and I received subpoenas to give depositions. All school records were included in the subpoenas. We left in one car at 5:00 A.M., because none of us had ever been to Lake County and we knew our drive would take about five hours. When we arrived in Crown Point, I called for final directions. A squad car was dispatched and led us to the Lake County Police Department.

Detective Ed Davies handled Loretta and Donna's depositions. Detective Decanter took my statements. I was relaxed in his presence, since I felt I was in friendly territory. My documentations were reassuring to me because I knew my answers to his questions were accurate.

As we drove away, I was in awe of the enormous complex. In the building next to the police department was the county jail where Dr. and Mrs. Shipley had been housed and held without bond since their arrest last November. The Lake County Courthouse was also on the premises.

During the long ride home, we discussed the bail hearing that was in progress. Since murder is not bondable in the state of Indiana, the evidence that was being introduced at the bail hearing would determine if the Shipleys would be freed before their jury trial. We mutually agreed they should remain in jail!

We wondered if any or all three of us would be subpoenaed, since there were fifty-four prospective witnesses who might be called. We knew Magistrate T. Edward Page, who was presiding at

43

the bail hearing, had recently ruled that Danielle would not testify due to the trauma for her in going against her father and stepmother as she faced them. I commented on how incensed I was after reading in the *Gary Post-Tribune* that Nick Thiros, Mrs. Shipley's attorney, had called Danielle a "little liar." His attack on a child really bothered me even though I realized this was in his plan to establish a question of Danielle's creditability to defend his client at the trial. We concurred that if Danielle had been called to testify in the summer of 1989 before the grand jury in Vincennes, there was a huge possibility we wouldn't be where we were today.

We talked about the custody fight that loomed over Danielle and Krista. Rhonda Shipley and her parents, Hope and Robert Hanlon, were on opposite sides in a battle for the children. I told my two companions that I had asked Detective Decanter about the girls earlier today. He said they were together in a fine foster home in Lake County. That was comforting, as was our arrival home after a most unusual day for this kindergarten teacher.

There were nine days of testimony in the bail hearing that were spaced over a period of five months. A list of fifteen witnesses told their side of the story to the magistrate. I was the only Vincennes school employee on that list.

Police officers testified of statements made by Dr. and Mrs. Shipley. These statements described Amy as living a tormented existence during the final months of her short life.

Both parents initially attributed Amy's death to her illness and more than twenty-five bruises on her body to a fall down patio stairs two days earlier. Then Dr. Shipley changed his statement, blurting to police that he had seen Gloria giving Amy a mouthful of black pepper the night before her death.

"Gloria was angry because Amy would not swallow it," Dr. Shipley stated. "Amy spit some of the pepper out of her mouth and Gloria got mad. I told her I would take Amy into the bathroom and give it to her."

Dr. Shipley contended that he did not force the child to swallow the noxious substance, but police found a can of pepper on the bathroom vanity. Mrs. Shipley told police Amy was forced to sleep in the bathroom almost every night for a month and a half prior to her death. She believed the youngster had tried to escape from the house to get food.

When police asked Dr. Shipley if it ever occurred to him Amy might have been hungry, he replied, "I thought about it, but I never really believed that's why she took the food."

Dr. Shipley passed the blame for Amy's punishments in his wife's lap. He related how they would often disagree with each other concerning the punishments for his daughters, but Gloria would threaten to leave if he would not administer beatings for trivial misconduct.

Mrs. Shipley portrayed herself as a loving mother who sat up with Amy comforting her the night before her death because she was suffering from a cold. She maintained Amy choked on toast the next morning and collapsed and, after numerous attempts to revive her, she had called an ambulance.

As testimony progressed, another decision relevant to the Shipley case was occurring. The *Sun-Commercial* was notified that it would get the grand jury transcripts under certain conditions. First, a jury had to be sequestered for the Shipley trial. Second, the Shipleys had to plead guilty or they had to be found guilty before the baffling proceedings in Vincennes would be told.

My turn as a witness finally arrived. On Easter Sunday, one of my close friends and a fellow teacher, Martha Harden, went with me to Crown Point. As we sat in our motel room that evening discussing the next day's events, I was flirting with nervousness. I did not know what to expect. I had been raised in a home of jurisprudence. My father had been an honorable attorney who stressed that it is better to stand up for something in which you believe than fall for anything. His teachings and my prayers carried me through the night.

Early the next morning Martha and I went to the courthouse and discovered that the hearing had been delayed until later in the day. Waiting is always difficult, but I kept "pretending" I was calm. We talked with Debbie and her mother, Dessie, and met Hope and Bob Hanlon for the first time. They impressed me as being sincerely concerned individuals who had been "kept in the dark" about their grandchildren by their former son-in-law and his second wife.

Finally, my name was called. I quickly entered and sat by myself at one end of a long rectangular table. Magistrate Page sat at the other end. Ms. Collins and Ms. Oliver were to my right. One of Dr. Shipley's attorneys, Dennis Zahn, sat to my left, with Dr. Shipley sitting directly behind him. Mrs. Shipley was beside her husband, and her attorney, Mr. Thiros, was also at the table. Debbie and several other reporters sat against the wall behind the deputy prosecutors. Martha, Dessie, and a few other spectators sat behind me.

When Mr. Zahn began questioning me, Dr. Shipley looked down at the floor and Mrs. Shipley stared at me. Mr. Zahn's approach was soft-spoken and I responded with the factual information as he asked for it. Mr. Thiros was a definite contrast to Mr. Zahn. He was louder and impatient and raised his voice in anger to some of my answers. I overheard Mrs. Shipley call me a liar on more than one occasion after I responded to her attorney's questions. I did my best to keep my composure as Mrs. Shipley glared at me when Mr. Thiros became more abrupt. Both attorneys questioned me on how I could remember dates and conversations from over two years ago. I explained that I had documented and saved my notes as my principal had suggested.

Mr. Thiros demonstrated his irritation with my response by yelling, "I would like to see those notes!"

I replied, "They are with the prosecutors."

That was our final exchange of conversation, and I was dismissed. The procedure had been a most stressful ordeal for me.

The thought of the trial seemed more frightening to me now after my experience at the bail hearing with Mrs. Shipley and Mr. Thiros. Regardless, I did not regret reporting Danielle's abuse, so I remained determined to continue telling all I knew about this case until justice was served.

Near the conclusion of the drawn-out hearing, there was a new decision that Danielle was now strong enough to testify. The media had dubbed Danielle the star witness for the prosecution. Because of the complexity of the evidence, Magistrate Page delayed the trial to August 5. The magistrate had intended to close the bail hearing the day of Danielle's testimony, since potential jurors were bound to read news accounts of it and could make up their minds about the Shipleys' innocence or guilt before the trial. But news media petitioned the court and he changed his mind.

During Danielle's testimony, she burst into tears after glancing at her father and stepmother, dressed in prison coveralls. The couple watched her without displaying emotion as she spoke about Amy and them.

Danielle told about Amy being punished for urinating on herself or stealing "junk" food from the kitchen. Danielle described an incident when a small piece of a brownie was missing from a pan of brownies. Their father discovered this and searched his three daughters' mouths with a toothbrush until he found brown crumbs inside Amy's mouth. Amy was spanked, hit, or forced to drink "yucky" milk laced with black pepper. She was primarily fed cereal while the rest of the family ate hamburgers and french fries. Amy was originally locked in one of the bathrooms when she climbed out a window and her father discovered it. Amy was then moved and locked inside a bathroom with no windows.

Danielle related her similar hardships while the family lived in Vincennes and Jasper. Not only was she required to drink "yucky" milk, but she was force-fed dishwashing soap to make her vomit.

The testimony of this fragile child rocked the state of Indiana with horror. Magistrate Page ruled the Shipleys would remain in jail without bond until their trial. Attorneys for the Shipleys, Dennis Zahn, James Voyles, and Nick Thiros, had been given an opportunity to see the hand of the prosecution to set the defense for their clients.

Part III
The Trial of
Dr. and Mrs. Gary Shipley

6

The Prosecution (August 5 to 14, 1991)

Debbie wanted to cover the trial, but she had reservations about asking her superiors to pay the costs of travel, food, and hotel expenses. However, money wasn't the only thing on her mind. As she had been raised in a rural community in southern Indiana and lived there most of her life, Lake County, near Chicago, seemed mammoth in size to her. But the fear of the unknown didn't stop her from asking the newspaper to send her. Her boss was receptive to the idea and placed faith in Debbie to relay the facts on a daily basis to her hometown community.

Not wanting to make the journey alone, Debbie decided to ask her mother to accompany her. Distorting her motive, Debbie approached the subject of enticing Dessie with all the "big city" would have to offer.

"It will be great," Debbie told her mother. "The hotel will have a hot tub in which you can relax, room service, you won't have to clean, and at night we can eat out and shop in an enormous mall. It'll be just like a vacation."

But Dessie was too smart. She knew that sleeping in a hotel room every night and missing home-cooked meals was not as luxurious as Debbie made it sound. She also realized there wouldn't be enough time to relax, enjoy the hot tub, and shop. But because she was on summer vacation from her job, she agreed to take the trip.

As Debbie packed, her nerves began to unravel. She had only

been to Lake County on one other occasion, when she reported on my testimony during the bail hearing. Most of the other bail hearing stories in the *Sun-Commercial* came from Bill Dolan, the reporter from the *Gary Post-Tribune* who had interviewed Mr. Ritterskamp and me the week after Amy died.

During the drive toward Lake County, Debbie wondered what the Shipleys would look like this time, how long the trial would last, and what the results would be. She had not been impressed with the defendants at the bail hearing. Both were dressed in jail clothing, which reminded her of hospital greens, and they did not appear to be clean or well groomed. They sat one chair apart and rolled their eyes at each other in disgust as testimony was given. Dr. Shipley was thin and his skin was pasty white. Mrs. Shipley was the exact opposite. She was definitely overweight, which made her look like she had four or five chins.

When Debbie arrived at the court building, she began to survey her surroundings. The modern building was situated between the Lake County jail and another county building. All three were connected by underground tunnels. Everyone who entered the court building had to pass through two metal detectors so that concealed weapons could be spotted. Once one was inside the courtroom, several rows of theaterlike seats were available. Dr. Shipley and his wife sat next to each other with their attorneys. The Shipleys appeared completely different than they did during the bail hearing. Dr. Shipley was wearing a nice suit and tie with a matching shirt while his wife wore a business suit and high-heeled shoes. Neither displayed fear as they talked with their lawyers during the jury selection. One by one, potential jurors were selected or eliminated for one reason or another. It was, as speculated, difficult to find impartial jurors because of the high-profile case. The screening process turned from hours into two and a half days, and finally, after lunch on August 7, the trial got under way.

Deputy prosecutors Sue Collins and Lillian Oliver looked to be in their early thirties. They appeared to be completely dedicated to the preservation of justice, having done their homework by preparing a list of fifty-four prospective witnesses. Their demeanor indicated from the opening of the trial that they were ready to fight for Amy's rights.

The first witnesses for the prosecution were Gary Vaughn and John Swanson, Lakes of the Four Seasons Fire Department emergency medical technicians. Their testimonies coincided. When they went in the door of the Shipley home, they followed a dark and cluttered hallway to where Amy was lying on the floor of the master bedroom. Her body was covered with bruises. Some were green, others were blue, and older bruises were yellow and fading. The child's eyes were sunken in their sockets, and the whites were red. Her skin was pale and cold. Amy had cold vomit in her hair, around her mouth, and on the blanket that half-covered her nude body. As the medical technicians cleaned the vomit out of her mouth, they noted that it was thick and full of pepper. All signs indicated the girl had been dead before help arrived. Several attempts were made to revive Amy, but medical workers could not get her to breathe and could not find a heartbeat.

A Merrillville paramedic, Timothy O'Brien, testified that he arrived at the scene within minutes. During cross-examination he stated that he had to inject Amy with an IV needle but could not find a vein that would take a sharp instrument. By this time Dr. Shipley had come home, and it was he who was able to get the needle in his daughter's body, on the third try.

Mr. O'Brien was grilled about the oxygen equipment he was using on the child.

"Isn't it true that Dr. Shipley told you the oxygen was not hooked up properly?" asked Mr. Voyles, one of Dr. Shipley's attorneys.

Although Mr. O'Brien conveyed that Amy was able to receive room air, which is about 21 percent pure oxygen, he hung his head when he verified that he had forgotten to hook up the oxygen tank to the mask strapped on Amy's face. It was then that Dr. and Mrs.

Shipley displayed looks of satisfaction on their faces, probably believing their attorney had scored a point with the jury.

Kay Sullivan, a nurse at the hospital where Amy had been taken, explained that she was in constant contact with the ambulance as it raced down the streets of Merrillville with sirens blaring. The nurse remembered Gloria Shipley had told her the child had fallen down a flight of carpeted steps.

"I just stared at the body in disbelief," declared Lois Miles, a medical social worker at Southlake Hospital, as she recalled seeing Amy's body in the trauma room. Ms. Miles said Gloria Shipley told her Amy had fallen outside on the deck the previous night.

All this testimony on the opening day of the trial was already making Debbie very uneasy. So far Amy's photographs had not been admitted into evidence. Debbie knew the two pathologists who had conducted autopsies on Amy were scheduled to be called as witnesses on behalf of the prosecution. A rumor around the courthouse was that the autopsy photographs were so graphic a secretary in the building had gone home ill after viewing them.

Dr. Young Kim of the Lake County Coroner's Office confirmed what Debbie had heard when he took the stand and exhibited the photographs of Amy. Spectators gasped and moaned as the photographs were revealed. Different sections of Amy's deceased body had been enlarged and bordered in black. Dr. and Mrs. Shipley didn't utter a sound or twinge a muscle as pictures of the child they had raised were shown. A stern look came over Judge Letsinger's face as he scolded the audience for their reactions. It was clear he did not want to take any chances of a jury being prejudiced, with the end result being a mistrial.

According to Dr. Kim, Amy had bruises all over her body caused by blunt force trauma. Their colors resembled those of the leaves on a tree during the autumn season. Amy was covered with varying shades of green, yellow, and brown. The most recent bruises stood out in vivid blue. Bruises also were prevalent on the top of her head. A burn mark was clearly visible on her right thigh, accompanied by another on her left foot. She also had hemorrhages near her small intestines. The child's eyes were sunken, which indicated dehydration, and she had a very small amount of fat tissue, which meant she was malnourished. During one of Amy's last breaths, she had inhaled vomit into her lungs, which contributed to her death.

A close-up of Amy seemed to be staring at Debbie. The emaciated girl's body featured wide-open eyes and matted hair. Her mouth was slightly open, as if she was trying to speak. A brown mark outlined her mouth, left there by an oxygen mask as emergency workers made a last effort to help her breathe. Her body looked as though skin had been stretched over a skeleton. The image of the girl tormented Debbie as she tried to concentrate on Dr. Kim's testimony.

The next day was no easier for Debbie, as Cathy Balon, who was employed in the crime lab at the Lake County Police Department, informed the court of what she had found in the trauma room with Amy's body. A pair of pink panties had been observed by Ms. Balon with writing on them telling the kind nature of "Friday's child." Debbie thought of how the words on the panties, "Loving and giving is Friday's child," seemed cryptic, because evidence revealed that Amy's last days were anything but kind.

Ms. Balon continued to explain what she had discovered as evidence the next day inside the Shipley home. Amy's room was cluttered with items that were out of place. The child's bed was disassembled and a cot appeared to be its replacement. Across the hall from Amy's room was a bathroom. A man's belt was found on the bathroom floor beside a child's sleeper. On the vanity were a pepper container, a bowl of what appeared to be spoiled cereal, cleaning supplies, a bottle of dishwashing liquid, and brownies. A brown substance around the drain of the bathtub was taken into evidence. The bottle of dishwashing liquid appeared to have brownie residue on it.

All of these items seemed strange to Debbie. Instead of toothpaste and a toothbrush, there were cleaning supplies and dishwashing liquid. And why were food items in the bathroom? Shouldn't they be kept in the kitchen? When a bolt lock was mentioned as being placed high on the outside of the door, which was out of the child's reach, Debbie experienced a cold chill going through her body, leaving her with goose bumps. She knew Amy had been a prisoner in her own home.

As Ms. Balon continued talking, the entire interior of the Shipley home became to seem even more bizarre. A photograph was entered into evidence showing boxes of cereal, a pan of brownies, and many other food items scattered across the countertop and kitchen table. It looked like someone had been on a feeding frenzy that led to the living room, where a loaf of bread was found on the floor.

A single brownie sat on a night table in the master bedroom along with multiple bottles of prescription medicines and syringes. One syringe still had a clear substance inside it while the other syringes had moisture residue. Two hairbrushes and another man's belt were part of the evidence police took from the master bedroom. The outside of the doorways leading to all the children's bedrooms had tape on them.

Defense attorneys questioned Ms. Balon as to why fingerprints were never taken from the pepper container. She replied that prints were found on the pepper container, but no attempt was made to determine whose prints they were. This bothered Debbie, and she also wondered why the brown substance in the tub and the contents of the syringes had not been tested.

Another witness to testify as to what the Shipleys had told him the day of Amy's death was Mark Malamatos, a Lake County deputy coroner. Mrs. Shipley told Mr. Malamatos that Amy was eating breakfast when she grabbed her throat and started flailing her arms. Dr. Shipley told him that the day of her death Amy hadn't wanted to eat before he went to work and appeared to be exhausted.

Other witnesses that day were pathologist Sharon Bulot, who explained the process of storing body fluids in the Coroner's Office; William Hubert, chief investigator in the Lake County Coroner's Office, who clarified the process of taking body fluids to and from the Office of Toxicology in Indianapolis; James Forbes, the superintendent in charge of drug analysis; and Jeff Retz, a laboratory supervisor with the Indiana State Department of Toxicology.

The following day's testimony began on an emotional high when Amy's maternal grandfather, Robert Hanlon, was called as a witness. With a pinched look on his face, Mr. Hanlon recounted in a quivering voice his last visit with his grandchild before her death. He said, "Amy was pale and thin and didn't play with the rest of the girls. She was usually the happy-go-lucky one of the three girls. At mealtime Amy was hungry and asked for seconds. We had been instructed by Gloria and Dr. Shipley not to give Amy second helpings. My wife and I did not give her more food because we were afraid if we had broken instructions, our visits would be cut out completely. We never had any trouble with any of the children gorging themselves on food. A year earlier Danielle had appeared as Amy did. She had lost a lot of hair and was pale."

Testifying after Mr. Hanlon were the last known people to see Amy alive besides the Shipley family. Approximately forty-eight hours before her death, two Crown Point teachers at the Alpha Learning Center had come into contact with Amy.

Renee Arnott was working the early shift on November 6, 1990, when Dr. Shipley brought Amy and Krista to the preschool and day care center. Amy was dressed in jeans and a long-sleeved shirt. She had dry patches of skin around her nose and her eyes and on her arms. Ms. Arnott said she did not examine Amy's arms any farther than the elbow. Amy followed Ms. Arnott most of the time and rarely played with other children.

When the shift at the day care center changed at 3:30 P.M., Debra Smith came on duty.

"Amy kept telling me she was hungry and thirsty," Ms. Smith stated.

At one point, Ms. Smith said she took Amy to the kitchen and gave her a graham cracker. She left Amy in the kitchen for a few minutes. When she returned, the child was crouched in a corner of the room with her back to the door. Amy looked startled when she saw her teacher.

"She had eaten a peanut butter sandwich I had left on the counter," Ms. Smith continued. "I picked her up and put her on my lap."

At that point, Ms. Smith noticed flakes in Amy's hair that resembled dandruff. Soon after, Dr. Shipley came to the day care center to pick up his daughters. That was the first and last time the teachers saw Amy alive.

The next witness was a pathologist from the Indiana University School of Medicine, Dr. Michael Clark, who reinforced the findings of Dr. Kim's first autopsy. Dr. Clark performed a second autopsy, which led him to believe poor physical health probably had stymied Amy's gag reflex. During an examination of the lungs, he saw that she had inhaled her stomach contents.

"Inhaling stomach contents is uncommon in children this age," Dr. Clark specified. "I don't think I've ever seen a five-year-old do that. The stomach contents were inhaled very close to the time of death. Ingesting black pepper could induce vomiting."

Dr. Clark reported that Amy's ankles were swollen, which is "a sign of profound malnutrition." Earlier witnesses testified that Dr. Shipley had told the hospital the girl's ankles were swollen because she suffered from arthritis.

"There were no signs of arthritis during the autopsy," Dr. Clark related.

Dr. Clark drew his conclusion that Amy was malnourished. Her eyes were sunken. She had no body fat either on the outside or around the internal organs. The child had about four folds of skin under her arms, which indicated she had lost a lot of weight.

Bruises were more extensive during the second autopsy because Dr. Clark pulled the scalp back farther than was done during the first autopsy. This enabled him to find bruises underneath the scalp and where the head met the neck. "The beaten, malnourished, and dehydrated condition of Amy's body discovered during the second autopsy added together and caused her to die," Dr. Clark concluded.

Dr. Stephen Coles, a forensic pathologist from Grand Rapids, Michigan, took the stand. He said he had written several articles on pepper inhalation.

"Pepper blocks the airway," Dr. Coles explained. "It is an irritant to the airway and could cause swelling. Because pepper is an irritant, it can cause vomiting and diarrhea."

Pulling out all the stops, the prosecution subpoenaed Dr. Cindy Christian, a pediatrician and employee of the Children's Hospital in Philadelphia, Pennsylvania. She was classified as an expert on children who had been sexually and physically abused.

Dr. Christian related, "I have been involved in a study of more than three hundred children who have fallen down stairs, and these children only suffered minor injuries. Less than 3 percent had injuries on their trunks and backs."

Previously submitted into evidence were the autopsy photographs from Dr. Kim that revealed Amy had bruises of all stages on most of her body. In Dr. Christian's opinion, Amy's bruises did not occur on a flight of stairs.

"There were too many different colors and they were too extensive," she said. "Amy's two internal hemorrhages could not have been caused from a fall down stairs."

In response to a statement made by Dr. Shipley at the time of his arrest, admitting to locking Amy in the bathroom at their home, Dr. Christian stated, "I would classify that as cruel punishment."

The Shipleys' attorneys had argued that Danielle, and later Amy, urinated and defecated on themselves in an attempt to manipulate their parents. Dr. Christian vigorously disputed that argument during cross-examination.

"I think when older children urinate and defecate on themselves," Dr. Christian said, "it's a sign of a serious emotional problem. If there are such severe emotional problems, it's an indication there's something wrong in that household."

This sensational murder trial was drawing an overflow of crowds. Citizens started filtering into the court building early and quickly filled each of the ninety-odd seats in Judge Letsinger's second-floor courtroom. As a result, bailiffs turned away would-be onlookers and posted a sign on the outside of the courtroom door announcing when there was no room left inside to sit.

"Curiosity," replied Elsie Zloza, when asked what had brought her to criminal court. She found the last vacant seat during the morning session of testimony. "I have always wanted to attend a hearing and didn't have the opportunity. Since I'm retired, I decided to attend this case," she explained.

Others had more personal reasons, like Mary Murrian, a single mother from Highland, Indiana, who was listening to her second day of testimony from a front-row seat. She was a junior pre-law student at Purdue University Calumet and planned to specialize in child abuse cases. "I'm a victim of child abuse," said Ms. Murrian. "If there would have been better information and advocates like there are now, I would have been spared ten years of sexual abuse."

Dora Thomason of Valpariso, Indiana, was a security guard for Lakes of the Four Seasons. She sent the emergency team to the Shipley home when Gloria Shipley called for help after Amy began choking.

"I just want to follow the case," Mrs. Thomason said.

Many in the gallery didn't need to hear the rest of the state's evidence to pronounce their verdict.

"In my book it was child abuse," responded Gloria Morris, a housewife from Schererville, Indiana.

"But was it murder?" she was asked.

"I can't say it was," Mrs. Morris replied. "I really can't say."

Michelle Kolvek, a seventeen-year-old staying with her grandparents in Cedar Lake, Indiana, was certain.

"I think abuse is murder," Miss Kolvek explained.

Miss Kolvek, who had been in the courtroom since the first day of testimony, said she had learned how to discipline her children in anticipation of when she becomes a parent.

"Not in the manner the Shipleys did it!" she exclaimed.

Some of these people had been attending the trial from the first day or even earlier, when jury selection began. Although most of their faces were friendly and Debbie talked with them, it wasn't the same as seeing people from her hometown. She was pleased when Ms. Oliver told her, "Patti will be called to the witness stand tomorrow."

Martha, who had accompanied me to the bail hearing, and I arrived at the hotel where Debbie and her mother were staying a few hours after Debbie found out I was coming. Dessie was tired from the "big city" life, so she stayed in her room while we met Debbie in the lobby. Although we did not discuss my forthcoming testimony, everyone knew the following day would be strained when I told the jury what I knew about the Shipley family.

When Martha and I arrived at the courthouse, my youngest son, Chad, and a college friend of his met us and became an additional support system for me. The boys went into the courtroom, and Martha stayed with me in the hall. She had decided earlier that morning not to be in court when I testified, because she thought she would become too angry at the defense attorneys, especially Mr. Thiros. As the bailiff led me to the witness stand to be sworn in, I was saying a silent prayer, asking that I would be strong and respond adequately.

Ms. Oliver directed her questions to me about my acquaintance with Danielle when she was a student in my classroom, using my testimony to show a pattern of child abuse on the part of the Shipleys long before Amy's death. During the cross-examination by the defense, I was surprised to find myself more at ease than the first time I was questioned by Mr. Zahn and Mr. Thiros at the bail hearing. I attribute this to my prayers being answered and to being somewhat familiar with the defense attorneys' personalities.

When Judge Letsinger excused me after more than an hour of questioning, I had a confident feeling that the jury knew I had told the truth and they believed me. I should have been experiencing contentment, since my participation in the trial was completed. Instead, I knew Danielle would eventually testify and I began to fret about her feelings and my anxiety about this courtroom situation for an eight-year-old child. The jury's verdict also was a major concern of mine.

Following me was Beth Thais, the Vincennes caseworker who had been assigned to Danielle. Her testimony was the first I was allowed to hear since my testimony had been given. I returned to the courtroom as a spectator with mixed emotions. The trial would be agonizing to watch, agonizing not to watch.

Mrs. Thais reinforced my statements concerning Danielle's abuse while she was in my kindergarten class. Because we had not seen each other since the day she removed Danielle from the Shipley home in 1989, I felt the jury could not help but believe Danielle was an abused child.

I was surprised during Mrs. Thais's testimony to finally receive an answer to a question I had frequently asked for two and a half years. How was the decision made to place Danielle from her short-term foster care of two weeks back into the Shipleys' home? Mrs. Thais stated that Danielle was placed back in her home on March 6, 1989, on a recommendation of Barbara Morgan, the clinical social worker.

I was not surprised when Mrs. Thais said Dr. Shipley would pull Danielle up by her hair when she had a temper tantrum. Danielle and I had not talked about how she had lost so much hair, but I was never convinced of her losing her hair only due to a hair disease.

Mrs. Thais testified that she had followed the case to Jasper when the Shipleys moved. Since Indiana is one of the few states that does not have a tracking system for child abusers, I had believed the Welfare Department was on top of this situation. My opinion changed rapidly when I heard her testimony that she had made only one home visit while the Shipleys lived in Jasper, because they lived there more than six months. Mrs. Thais also explained that other visits were made in parks or restaurants. I asked myself how Mrs. Thais would be able to tell if Danielle had been physically abused while visiting the family in a public place. She would not be at liberty to examine Danielle's skin for bruises under her clothing.

Mrs. Thais said attempts were made to get Dubois County Welfare in Jasper to monitor the case, but officials at that agency were not willing to do so. Debbie later related a discrepancy to me, as she had spoken with the director of the Dubois County Welfare Department, John Pavelka, during an interview for a pretrial story. He said no Vincennes agency had warned him of the matter and he had become aware of the Shipley family through the public school system in Jasper.

"To my knowledge, I was not directly contacted by another government agency other than the school," Mr. Pavelka stated to Debbie.

Mrs. Thais's testimony ended by telling the court that the wardship of the Welfare Department was dismissed by Knox County Superior Court judge Theobald early in 1990. She said he did so even after the Welfare Department requested the wardship continue. She needed wardship to continue because Danielle was going to be admitted to the Evansville Children's Psychiatric Center and she wanted to make sure Danielle remained there long enough for treatment.

The next witness was Pamela Dewey-Pugh, Danielle's therapist at the Evansville Children's Psychiatric Center. Mrs. Dewey-Pugh recollected the months she treated her patient, telling jurors that Danielle displayed few problems during her stay at the center. She never "binged" on food or defecated on herself. In the first few weeks of her stay, Danielle did wet the bed on occasion, but this was not unusual for a new patient.

The therapist said, "The Shipleys informed me Danielle was rebellious and would steal food. Dr. Shipley said he made Danielle drink dish soap and syrup of ipecac to make her throw up the food she had eaten. Gloria Shipley once told me Danielle wasn't given the opportunity to act out in the hospital and that officials needed to set up situations for her to steal food."

Mrs. Dewey-Pugh related that Danielle was concerned that if she gained weight her parents wouldn't love her. She stated that Danielle was obsessed with food, calories, and exercise and she had advised the Shipleys to "back off" the subject.

There were times after Danielle arrived at the center, Mrs. Dewey-Pugh said, that she had difficulty locating the girl's parents to discuss Danielle with them. After one home visit, Danielle returned quite upset, telling how she was forced to take cold showers. Also, Danielle told how she had to sit with her arms and legs outstretched in space while riding in the car during the long trip back to the center. When Mrs. Dewey-Pugh completed her descriptions of the abusive treatments of Danielle, eight-year-old Danielle supplied the details about Amy's misery as she took the next oath to testify.

After the prosecutors announced the child's name, Danielle Nicole Shipley, the courtroom began to buzz but quickly became quiet when Judge Letsinger gave the audience a disapproving scowl. Danielle entered the courtroom by the jury entrance to avoid walking through a courtroom packed with spectators. She scampered to her seat, her head barely clearing the rail of the witness stand.

This was the first time I had seen Danielle since Saint

Patrick's Day in 1989. Gone was the pixie haircut and the thin, frail features I had seen more than two years ago. Her hair was lighter, longer, and pulled back with a headband. She looked healthy in her pink jumper and white blouse with pink polka dots. I wasn't surprised that Danielle wore pink, as I remembered it being her favorite color in kindergarten. I was delighted with her overall appearance and joyous that she was alive. This verbal public display would soon be over for her, and after the testimony she should be able to continue to heal.

She was carefully guided through her testimony by Deputy Prosecutor Oliver, describing the torturous punishments doled out to Danielle's five-year-old sister in the months before her death.

Danielle's first response to the deputy prosecutor was when she said, "Amy slept in the bathroom because she always pottied her pants."

Danielle explained that one of the rules the Shipleys enforced was that Amy had to have three days and nights dry before she could sleep on a cot in her bedroom. Amy never made it to her room. She was made to sleep at night in a locked bathroom. If Amy had "a mess" in the bathroom, she cleaned it up herself. A bottle of Mr. Clean and a rag were kept in the bathroom.

One time Amy crawled out a window in a different bathroom just off the kitchen. Her father found her and put a broom in front of that bathroom window and tape on the door knob. At times, Danielle was instructed to lock her sister inside a bathroom across the hall from Amy's bedroom.

"Amy drank formula," Danielle said. "My mom and dad gave her formula," Danielle testified.

She said they would spoon pepper into a liquid formula, which she called "yucky milk," and make Amy drink it. Sometimes she had to drink "yucky milk," too. Also, there were times when Amy was forced to watch everyone else in the family eat at the dinner table.

Danielle related an incident that had occurred one week before Amy's death. Krista and Danielle were allowed to dress for Halloween and trick-or-treat. Amy was not. She was taken in the car with her parents to watch her sisters enjoy the fun. When they all went home, Amy had to watch her two sisters eat their candy.

Danielle said she and Amy had to take cold showers and "ice baths," in which ice cubes were added to cold water. She testified that occasionally she had to watch her younger sister taking a cold bath.

"Sometimes Gary or Gloria would watch her. Sometimes I did, just to make sure she didn't get out," Danielle stated.

Danielle told of how the children were punished for lying.

Ms. Oliver asked, "What did you drink?"

"Dis...dis...," Danielle paused as she stuck out her tongue as if it were tied and took a deep breath. "Dish soap. Mom and Dad would hold our heads back. We had to swallow it."

"How did it make you feel?" Ms. Oliver said.

"Gross," Danielle replied.

Danielle told of Krista, Amy, and she having to stand in a corner. She said they would bend over with their hands down or behind their backs. They were spanked with belts, hands, hairbrushes, and a piece of wood from their couch. She also testified that her father and stepmother would "smack our feet" when they were bad.

"Krista, I think, me, and Amy had to sit on the floor with our feet up. Once we might have had socks on. We never had shoes on," she said.

Danielle said she and her father made brownies the night before Amy died. He ate one and came back for another, she explained, when he noticed "a little bite gone." He began trying to find out who had eaten the brownie and broken the house rule "you can't steal." She continued by telling how their father had forced their mouths open wide and checked their teeth for food. "Amy's had brown stuff," she said.

As punishment, Danielle told how Amy had to get her tooth-

66

brush and how their father "took the toothbrush and started scrubbing on the back teeth."

Danielle spoke of another incident that happened the night before Amy died. She saw Amy running through the house with a piece of bread and then hiding behind a chair in the living room.

She said, "I told my dad . . . because that was one of the rules. If we saw Amy with something, we had to tell."

On the morning Amy died, Danielle said she went to school and remembered little about the day. She stated she did not remember Amy falling at home. She also said Amy was not allowed to go outside and play.

Near the end of the eighty-five minutes on the witness stand, Danielle squirmed and tugged at her hair as she concluded the chilling accounts of beatings, taking icy baths, and drinking concoctions of milk laced with black pepper that were a daily part of her home life before her younger sister died. But Danielle never cried, remaining alert and well composed for her age. She calmly answered the cross-examination by two of the three defense attorneys, Mr. Zahn and Mr. Thiros, for the final thirty minutes.

Since Danielle was the last of the twenty-five witnesses called by Deputy Prosecutors Collins and Oliver, the state's case was rested after six days of testimony.

Outside the jurors' presence, the couple's defense attorneys asked Judge Letsinger to dismiss the murder charge after stating the prosecution had failed to provide enough evidence to show intent to kill the child.

"There's no evidence, Judge, these people ever intended to do anything except discipline a child, and this is not murder," Mr. Thiros said.

"What direct evidence is there of any intent to kill?" the judge asked Ms. Collins.

He repeated the question twice, chastised Ms. Collins, then ordered her to sit down after he felt she failed to tell which part of the prosecution's case addressed the issue of "knowingly intended" to kill Amy. Ms. Collins had said the child's poor physical condition and the force-feedings of pepper showed the Shipleys' intent to harm Amy.

As I was listening to the debate initiated by the defense to dismiss the murder charge, Sally Haviar, the director of the Victim Witness Assistance Program, approached the row where I was sitting and motioned for me to come outside the courtroom. She took me to the prosecuting attorney's office to be with Danielle. As we embraced, I batted my eyes a few times to refrain from freeing a waterfall of tears.

Bob Hanlon introduced me to Danielle's mother, Rhonda. I had recently learned that the Hanlons had dropped their custody suit and Rhonda had Danielle and Krista living with her in Indianapolis. I was delighted with the apparent harmony between the three generations in the room.

Even though I hadn't been sure I would get a chance to be with Danielle, I had brought surprises for the two girls. I went to get them, and Danielle opened hers in record time, assuring me she would deliver Krista's packages. During our half-hour reunion of quality time, Danielle and I chatted about her school, smiled a lot, and hugged some more.

As I climbed the stairs to return to the court session, I now had better "vibes" about Danielle's future. She had already exhibited that she was a fighter, as her will to survive had helped her live through extremely difficult times in her young life. I recalled an article Debbie wrote last January that was published in our newspaper after she had an interview with the director of a preschool and child care center Danielle attended in 1989. One quote stuck in my memory.

"She [Danielle] would have eaten the wallpaper to survive," said Sue Adams, director of Kinder Horizons in Jasper.

Because she was a proven survivor, a stable home life, family love, and therapy held my hopes high for providing Danielle with opportunities for safe and natural experiences as she continued to develop into womanhood.

I reentered the courtroom and just as I sank into a seat, Judge Letsinger said the prosecution had presented only a "modicum of evidence" to prove murder, but he denied the request of the defense and adjourned his court for the day. I left emotionally exhausted but eager to share Danielle's visit with my friends.

7

The Defense (August 15 to 19, 1991)

Dennis Zahn and James Voyles, who represented Dr. Shipley, were law partners from Indianapolis. Mr. Zahn was slim and mild-mannered while his partner was husky and boyish looking. They were known in legal circles as intense professionals who, through investigative skills, hard work, and courtroom dramatics, gave their best for clients. Gloria Shipley's attorney, Nick Thiros of Merrillville, was balding, robust, and assertive. He was known as the best lawyer money could buy in northern Indiana.

The defense began its case by calling counselor Dan Jackson, who had been employed at the Southern Hills Counseling Center in Jasper until October 1990. While he was employed there, the Shipleys were his clients, beginning treatment in the last half of 1989. Mr. Jackson said he counseled the family twenty-seven times but saw Danielle eight times by herself.

"All during the treatment the Shipleys told me they were leaving," he testified. "I didn't think it was fair to form a therapeutic relationship with Danielle."

One recommendation Mr. Jackson said he made to the Shipleys to modify Danielle's behavior was a "time-out" procedure in which attention was removed from the child's behavior. He suggested a bathroom be used for a "time-out" area. In the forced-cycle technique, the child had the option of staying in the bathroom or coming out and performing the task that had caused the parents to send her to the bathroom in the first place. Mr. Jackson said he never recommended placing a lock on the door with the child inside the room.

During therapy with Danielle, he diagnosed her as being oppositional, defiant, in a major state of depression, and experiencing a parent-child problem. In a situation such as the Shipleys', where there was accusation of an eating disorder, emphasis should be taken off food and eating should be made a "normal experience." Mr. Jackson related that he was very explicit to the Shipleys that physical punishment would not be appropriate.

Gloria Shipley's parents, Irma and Don Pfleiderer of Danville, Illinois, were the next witnesses for the defense. Both said the Shipley children were affectionate to their daughter and had been involved in the wedding ceremony of Gary and Gloria.

Each testified that Danielle "stole" food while visiting them. They stated that they never saw Gary or Gloria physically hurt any of the children.

Mr. Pfleiderer related, "Danielle was moody and wore diapers at their home because of potty problems."

"Time-out was the only method of discipline witnessed at our home," Mrs. Pfleiderer said.

When he testified in his defense, Dr. Shipley was not as composed as his daughter had been a day earlier. With his voice shaking and eyes tearing he described his children's behavior problems and his difficulty dealing with the situations.

He first testified about conduct problems with his oldest daughter, Danielle. He noticed her being defiant and writing on the walls and furniture at their home in Vincennes during the first half of 1987.

Dr. Shipley related, "Her behavior changed for the better in the middle of October 1987. We didn't have a lot of problems until after Gloria and I were married." He would try to talk to Danielle and get her to go to her room. He said, "When she was ready to do what we wanted her to do, she could come out."

In the summer of 1988, Danielle began getting out of bed in the middle of the night.

"Things were not always where we left them," he stated. "The salt and pepper shakers were clogged. Things were out of place. We found dishes that were clean, but not where we left them. We tried to talk to Danielle, but she denied it. I would imagine Gloria did most of the talking."

The first thing they did to catch Danielle "stealing food" was put tape on the refrigerator door. "It was broken," said Dr. Shipley, "and she admitted it at that point. We hoped by talking with her she would quit."

Then Danielle learned how to put the tape back on the door where she had removed it. Danielle also began to "act out." She would steal from her sisters and refuse to do chores assigned by her parents. She would stand in the middle of the floor and scream. Dr. Shipley recalled that the first time he spanked Danielle was in the fall of 1988.

"I began to use a paint stirrer because my hand left red marks and a paint stirrer wouldn't. Sometimes Danielle would go weeks without a spanking. Other times I would spank her daily—sometimes more," he explained.

Danielle's conduct became worse. She would potty on the floor or "anywhere she felt like it."

Trying to discredit Danielle, Dr. Shipley explained to the jury the hot-water problems he and his family encountered in their Vincennes home. He spoke specifically about one occasion when Danielle did not want to take a family trip. When she refused to help put the belongings in the car, she "pottied" her pants. After being told to take a second shower to cleanse herself, the water came out cold because everyone else in the family had used the shower. "I never purposely gave her a cold shower," he declared.

After Thanksgiving of 1988, Dr. Shipley began noticing Danielle's hair loss. In December, Danielle was taken to a dermatologist in Vincennes. He diagnosed Danielle as having a common type of hair disease with an unknown cause that could last a few days, months, or years.

"I would pull her pigtails but would never pull out clumps of hair," Dr. Shipley said.*

By January, Danielle's hair loss had become worse. When she was taken back to see the dermatologist, he prescribed an ointment to put on her hair to stimulate certain cells.

"She looked horrible," Dr. Shipley related.

A week before Danielle was removed from the Shipley home, Dr. Shipley said, she was having a "fit" in the hallway at their house. He told Danielle to go to her bedroom and threatened to spank her if she refused. When she would not go to her room, he began to hit her with a paint stirrer as she covered herself with her hands. "She was screaming and kicking," he said. "I just kept smacking her thighs."

Danielle was removed at that time from the Shipley home after bruises were noticed at school. One of the conditions Dr. Shipley said he had to meet to get Danielle back was talking with Barbara Morgan, a clinical social worker in Vincennes. He explained, "The first time we met, she tried to calm us down. She told us to come back next week and if things went as well as they had been, she would recommend Danielle be back in our home."

The Shipleys continued to see Mrs. Morgan until June. She made suggestions to help them with their problem.

"Once we left Vincennes, there were marked improvements. The kids liked Jasper and the area," he said.

Then the Shipleys began to see food disappear again. Danielle was starting to get out of bed and "steal" food.

"She would say things to upset her sisters and coax them into taking Popsicles into the playroom, then tell us," Dr. Shipley related.

---

*During this time frame, Danielle was in my kindergarten class. She could never wear pigtails because her hair was always cut short in a pixie haircut.

One time Danielle ate sausage that had been left in the family van. Because the food was old, she became ill. Another time she got into the trash to eat some old gravy. Her parents gave her syrup of ipecac to make her vomit.

When Mrs. Morgan was asked for a counseling referral in Jasper, she recommended Dan Jackson. By this time, Danielle had begun to defecate on herself again, then smear it on the walls. Mr. Jackson said Danielle wanted more control. He suggested she be sent to "time-out" until she was ready to come out by herself. Although Mr. Jackson did not give the Shipleys a time frame to leave Danielle in this isolated area she began to stay in the bathroom for five to six hours. At meals Danielle would be allowed out of the bathroom, and then she would be put back in until bedtime. At that time she would be permitted to go to her room.

Dr. Shipley said, "That was a problem. She would be left there until she was ready. It was a constant uproar. Danielle could be in a great mood; then if she didn't want to go somewhere, she'd go to the bathroom."

After Dr. Shipley testified that Mr. Jackson had told him to calmly instruct Danielle to clean up her own messes, his voice rose and he began to cry.

"Dan, that sounds so easy to do, but it's not," he said, as if he were speaking to Mr. Jackson.

After various recommendations from Mr. Jackson, the decision was made to hospitalize Danielle at the Evansville Children's Psychiatric Center. Danielle had two home visits before Dr. Shipley was admitted for a severe asthma attack at an Indianapolis hospital.

"I couldn't breathe and Gloria called an ambulance," he recalled.

During his stay at the hospital from June 16 to July 2, 1990, Dr. Shipley remembered being placed on a ventilator to help him with his breathing problems. Danielle was discharged from the

Evansville center during her father's hospital stay. When he was dismissed from the hospital, the Shipleys lived at the apartment of his ex-wife, Rhonda, in Indianapolis. From there the family moved to Gloria's parents' home in Danville, Illinois, until August 18. The family stayed at various hotels until they moved into a rented home on September 15, at Lakes of the Four Seasons, on the outskirts of Crown Point.

While living there, Dr. Shipley said he began to see traits in Amy that he had observed with Danielle. Amy was stubborn and in an effort to catch her sneaking out of her room at night to "steal" food, the Shipleys began putting tape on her bedroom doorknob.

"Her potty problems began at Rhonda's apartment," stated Dr. Shipley. "Amy slept in her room on a cot. She always had problems pottying at night, but no blame was placed on her. It really upset her when it happened."

For disciplining Amy, the Shipleys tried the same things they had used with Danielle. He described short "time-outs" in a corner. An example he gave was five or six minutes at once, but never more than a couple of hours.

Amy was placed in one of two bathrooms during the night. When the Shipleys realized Amy was getting out at night, they put a broom under the doorknob so it would fall if she left the bathroom.

"We told her," Dr. Shipley said, "if she slept in the bathroom, it wouldn't bother her that much to go to the bathroom. We used a king-size comforter for her to sleep on. We wouldn't close the door until midnight, when we went to bed. We would get her up several times in the night to go to the bathroom."

Dr. Shipley related that by this time he and his wife were spanking the children again with their hands or hair brushes. "Amy and Krista were getting spanked the most, but whenever Danielle was hit, all three girls were punished," he stated.

Amy's parents were trying to control her eating habits. At first

Amy was fed cereal with bran and nuts because they believed she wouldn't like it, but she did. They tried to make the cereal taste bad by putting pepper in it.

Dr. Shipley said, "She didn't even act like it was there. Then we gave her a basic formula that provided all the nutrients she needed."

One month before Amy died, the Shipleys began to use a belt on her as punishment.

"We didn't tell anyone what was going on unless we felt like they could help us. We didn't feel like they needed to know. Danielle used to beg us not to tell," he stated.

As the defense continued leading Dr. Shipley through his testimony, he said he was at home two nights before Amy's death when she fell down wooden deck stairs. Amy had started to the car to get papers out of it that she had brought home from day care.

"Gloria and I were in the kitchen when we heard loud crying," he recalled. "She had fallen down ten or twelve wooden stairs and complained a little bit. She showed no signs of significant injuries."

Dr. Shipley remembered that when he came home from work the next day, Amy looked like she didn't feel good. When he asked her if she wanted anything to eat, she replied that she wasn't hungry. Shortly after their brief conversation, Dr. Shipley discovered some candy was missing from the house. "Just tell us the truth," Dr. Shipley had said to Amy. "Just don't lie to us."

He then went to Danielle, who, in Dr. Shipley's opinion, looked like she had gained weight because her clothes were not fitting well.

"We talked to her for about one half hour," he said. "She admitted taking the candy but was eating it at the bus stop."

Ten or fifteen minutes after their talk, Danielle returned to her parents' room and said Amy was eating a piece of bread in the living room. Gloria called to Amy and she came from the living room, holding an empty bag that had once contained pastries.

"I told her I'd have to spank her. I did so six times on her bottom and she left the room. Then, I heard her throwing up in the bathroom," he related.

While Amy was sick, Gloria was in Danielle's bedroom, where she found fifteen or twenty candy wrappers in a bottom dresser drawer.

Dr. Shipley said, "I grabbed her [Danielle's] arm. I told Danielle it was her fault Amy was doing all this stuff. She got mad. Danielle looked like the old Danielle. Then I went to my bathroom. I could hear Danielle singing, 'Amy's eating pepper.' Then I heard someone say, 'Just swallow it, Amy.'"

When he exited the bathroom and entered the master bedroom, he told Amy to give him the can of pepper she was holding. She had pepper outlining her mouth and on the inside of her upper lip. Dr. Shipley said he then walked Amy to her bathroom and set the can of pepper on the bathroom sink.

"That night she sounded like she was croupy. I would wake her up many times in the night," he recalled.

The next morning Dr. Shipley found diarrhea on Amy's legs, her hair, her comforter, and the bathroom floor. He threw the comforter in the washer and washed up her mess.

"She looked like she had a horrible flu bug," explained Dr. Shipley. "I saw the bruises, but I didn't pay much attention to them because I assumed they were from the fall."

Dr. Shipley said he fixed Amy oatmeal and milk for breakfast, but when he took it to her in the bathroom, she was leaning over the sink. "She didn't want anything," he said. "I left it there."

When Dr. Shipley left for work, he said, Gloria was still in bed. He remembered calling his wife about 10:00 A.M., at which time they decided if Amy hadn't eaten anything by lunch she would be taken to a doctor. Gloria called him at the clinic a half hour later to report that Amy's condition had worsened. He left the clinic for home. When he arrived there about 11:00 A.M., he saw emergency vehicles parked outside his house. He met Gloria in the hall.

"Gloria said, 'Amy's in full arrest,'" he stated.

In the master bedroom, he saw Amy lying on the floor with emergency workers performing CPR on her. Gloria told him Amy had choked on a piece of toast.

"Gloria came back down the hall and kept saying, 'We've got to get her back. We can't lose her,' I knew the only chance she had was for me to calm down," he related.

He walked into the kitchen, and after a short time he came to the conclusion that emergency workers could not adequately resuscitate Amy.

"You have to get them back as quickly as you can to prevent brain damage. I stood by the door and prayed he could get the [IV] tube in," Dr. Shipley said.

When paramedics couldn't get the IV into her frail arm, Dr. Shipley said he was able to get one in his daughter's neck.

"I told them to watch the oxygen when they got ready to move her to take her to the hospital. But the tube was just lying there," he recalled.

Dr. Shipley explained that the most important element to reviving someone is oxygen and the paramedic had forgotten to hook up the tube to the tank. After the tank was properly hooked up and the child was inside the ambulance, Dr. Shipley and his wife followed the ambulance to the hospital in their car.

At the time Amy collapsed, she had a painkiller in her bloodstream. He said he did not know Amy had the drug in her system until an autopsy was performed later.

"Thinking back, she looked like someone who was on narcotics," he noted with a puzzled look on his face. "Narcotics do depress gag reflexes. She looked like she was half-asleep sitting on the toilet when I left for work that morning."

After Ms. Collins had her turn cross-examining Dr. Shipley,

further testimony was taken by the defense attorneys.

"In Vincennes, when Danielle would stand and stare, we'd say, 'Danielle, just run out to the barn and back until you calm down.' We didn't want to smack Danielle's face, but we did occasionally. When all three were arguing, we'd smack them in the head just to get them to step back," Dr. Shipley stated.

He defended his wife on the witness stand. He admitted Gloria was furious with him when he yelled at the children.

"She'd go off by herself," said Dr. Shipley. "Then Gloria told me to make a list of punishments to use. The only way we could cope with it was together. You were always scared what was going to happen."

The defense attorneys questioned Dr. Shipley about a statement he had made to police following his arrest. The statement said that he had seen Gloria give Amy a mouthful of pepper the night before her death.

"Amy had the pepper," he said in court. "Gloria wasn't even near her. I never saw Gloria do anything to harm the children."

When the defense attorneys believed they had gotten what they needed from Dr. Shipley, it was Ms. Collins's turn again, as tension filled the air.

Questioning from the prosecution started with the time when Gloria became a part of the Shipley family. Dr. Shipley said his ex-wife and Gloria were basically friends when Rhonda left the marriage.

"What was your relationship with Gloria and Rhonda?" Ms. Collins asked.

Mr. Thiros and Mr. Voyles jumped from their seats and objected to the question. Whispers filled the courtroom.

"There has been no evidence these children were affected by these suggestions," Mr. Thiros told the judge.

"Was there sex between you and Gloria before your marriage?" Ms. Collins asked Dr. Shipley.

"No," he replied.

Ms. Collins said, "Did the relationship between Gloria and Rhonda change?"

"They were real good friends at that point," Dr. Shipley responded.

"Did you take out a safe-deposit box?" she asked.

"Six weeks after Rhonda left, I was advised to write things down. Rhonda told me she didn't want to get divorced from me because she felt the kids and Gloria had been stolen from her," he answered.

"Was there ever a time when this relationship between Gloria and Rhonda was going on while the family was living together?" Ms. Collins asked.

"Yes," he replied with his head hanging down. "Rhonda didn't want to be married. She didn't want the kids and me. She just wanted Gloria."

The silence in the courtroom was so strong a pin could have been heard dropping. But just as suddenly as Ms. Collins started this line of questioning, she changed the subject and began asking Dr. Shipley about signs of dehydration in humans. Dr. Shipley said he had seen dehydration in many of his patients while practicing medicine. He explained what happens when people do not get adequate fluids, then said he did not believe Amy was in need of medication. He denied that Amy had lost a lot of weight but after viewing a photograph of his child's body said she might have lost "some weight."

"This child looks sick to you, doesn't she?" Ms. Collins fired at Dr. Shipley.

"Yes, ma'am," he replied in a quiet tone.

In an effort to help sway the jury toward the prosecution's side, Ms. Collins asked Dr. Shipley to tell how their family pets were treated. Food and water were left out overnight for their cats and they could roam the house whenever they wanted, unlike Amy, who was kept in a locked bathroom, Ms. Collins noted.

Sometimes the family dog would sleep in the bedroom with "the girls."

In an agitated tone, Ms. Collins began to drill Dr. Shipley about the brownies he and Danielle had baked the night before Amy's death.

"Did you eat a brownie?" she asked.

"Yes," he replied.

"Did you steal another?" she rapidly asked.

"I don't know what you mean," Dr. Shipley said.

"How many brownies did you have that night?" she fired again.

"I could have had quite a few," he responded.

"But you certainly didn't steal any, did you?" Ms. Collins asked in a sarcastic tone.

"No," he replied.

Ms. Collins switched gears and once again brought out the photographs of Amy's body.

Dr. Shipley sat emotionless as he used a pointer on the photographs to show what he believed to be signs of dehydration, malnutrition, and physical abuse on the different parts of Amy's body. As he clinically pointed to the signs in a professional manner, Gloria sat at the defense table jotting down notes.

Dr. Shipley's testimony concluded when Ms. Collins asked the doctor about a statement he made the night after his arrest.

"According to the statement," said Ms. Collins, "you saw your wife give Amy a mouthful of dry black pepper. Gloria became angry when the child would not swallow it."

"I was just rambling that day," he replied.

Debbie had become exhausted during Dr. Shipley's testimony trying to write every detail as well as the reactions of those around her. When the defense attorneys said they had one more witness for the day who had traveled from southern Indiana to testify, her heart sank.

Louis Vaught of Scottsburg had made the journey to tell the

jury what he knew about the Shipley family. He was currently involved with a family-owned pest control business, but in October 1990 he was a hospital administrator at a North Vernon facility. He met Dr. Shipley while he was working in the emergency room at the hospital.

On a fall day a few weeks before Amy's death, the Shipley family was in North Vernon to have lunch with Mr. Vaught and tour homes that were for sale. Mr. Vaught noticed that Amy had a scratch on her nose. When he asked the girl what had happened, Gloria interjected that Amy had been in a fight with her sisters. He did not remember seeing any other marks on Amy.

During cross-examination, Mr. Vaught said that Amy's legs were covered with opaque hose and her arms were covered with a long-sleeved shirt.

The following day began with Gloria Shipley taking the stand. Much of what she had to say about how she met the Shipley family had been introduced to the jury during Dr. Shipley's testimony. In July 1987, the Shipleys had moved to Vincennes, at which time Gloria was working at Scott Paper Company in Louisville, Kentucky. In August or September of that year, she moved back into the Shipley home to take care of the children.

"I felt real close to all of them," she said. "Krista almost felt like my own."

Shortly after Rhonda left and admitted herself to a psychiatric hospital in Indiana, Gloria and Gary began to use discipline on the children. "We had the girls stand in a corner as a form of discipline or go to bed early," she noted.

Amy began picking up bad habits from Danielle, such as lying or stealing food. After they had rented the Lakes of the Four Seasons home, Amy would stay awake until she thought everyone was asleep, then get up and steal food. Gloria also discussed two occasions on which she had to induce vomiting in Amy because she had eaten rotten food. The first time she was given "syrup of ipecac," but it didn't work. The second time she was given dishwashing soap on the advice of a pediatrician in Jasper, Gloria said. Amy would eat at inappropriate times. When it was time to eat regular food, she would not eat or would sit at the table, eat, and then vomit. Gloria described another eating event that involved Danielle. She had eaten a box of snacks, then vomited in her bed and slept in it.

When testifying about the night before Amy's death, Gloria said that she had been up several times with the child, who was sleeping in the bathroom with the door open.

"At one point I rocked her for about an hour and a half," she testified.

Amy had a stomachache and a headache, so Gloria gave her some Tylenol. She denied giving her dry pepper.

The day of Amy's death, Gloria said, Amy slept for a while on her sleeping bag in the master bedroom, then got into bed with her. When Krista got up, Gloria went to the kitchen to fix breakfast. She said she closely supervised Amy that morning. While fixing breakfast, she heard a noise in the bathroom, which she believed was Amy falling in the shower. When she went to check, Amy denied that she had fallen.

After Amy was done in the bathroom, she went to the kitchen to eat some toast and drink a liquid milk formula mixture. Amy began to wave her arms and had tears running down her face. Gloria believed the child was choking and tried the Heimlich maneuver to dislodge the food. She took Amy to the master bedroom and grabbed a stethoscope but could not hear a heartbeat. She then called the ambulance.

"Did you do anything to kill that child?" asked Mr. Thiros.

"No," she sobbed.

During cross-examination, Gloria denied giving Amy the narcotic painkiller or a mouthful of dry pepper.

Gloria said, "We talked about using salt, but we were afraid too much would hurt her."

About two weeks before Amy's death Gloria said she and her

husband stopped using pepper because it was not doing any good. The idea behind giving the child pepper was so she would dislike the liquid formula and cereal and would eat nutritious food.

When Gloria was shown a picture of Amy's body taken during an autopsy, Deputy Prosecutor Oliver pointed to several "marks." One, which appeared to be a burn, Gloria said she had not noticed. Gloria also said she did not notice a mark that appeared to be a needle injection.

As Gloria looked at a picture of Amy's protruding ribs, she said, "Her ribs were always visible to a certain extent."

She stated that Amy was not malnourished and looked healthy a few days before her death. She said she doubted the findings of two pathologists as to the cause of Amy's death and did not remember Amy appearing as she did in the autopsy photographs.

Ms. Oliver then began to question Gloria about her relationships.

"Did you have sex with Gary?" Ms. Oliver asked.

"Not before we were married," Gloria answered.

"Did you have sex with Rhonda?" asked Ms. Oliver.

"If you are implying lesbianism, I am no more a lesbian than you are," Gloria replied.

After a long time on the witness stand and denial of the accusations put before her, Gloria stepped down and resumed her seat next to her husband.

The prosecution then called a rebuttal witness, Roger Maickel, a pharmacologist at Purdue University. He said he had reviewed the blood levels of the narcotic in Amy at the time her autopsy was performed. He testified that the level found was not high enough to be lethally toxic, but that it could have been injected about one to two hours before it was measured. He explained that the side effects of an "overdose" of this drug, Darvocet, included nausea, vomiting, dizziness, and respiratory depression, which meant the slowing down of breathing. Mr. Maickel was the final witness to testify during the Shipley trial.

8

Closing Arguments (August 20, 1991)

Deputy Prosecutor Collins began the closing arguments by telling the jury that when Danielle was taken out of her home, Dr. Shipley and Gloria turned their attention to Amy. She stated, "They starved her. They beat her. They eventually killed her. Isn't it interesting that two medical people knew where to beat the children where it was not easily detected and in areas where it was the most sensitive?"

Ms. Collins said that Amy wasted away before their eyes and died a slow, torturous death. She told the jurors, "This couple was charged with neglect for the way Amy Shipley lived, murder for the way Amy Shipley died."

She explained that there would be several charges on which the Shipleys could be convicted. One option would be involuntary manslaughter, which was a battery that resulted in death but with no intent to kill.

"This is not one act. They started to kill Amy before November 8," Ms. Collins declared.

Another option would be reckless homicide, which was when a person embarked on a course that resulted in death without intending to kill. The other option would be murder, where there was intent or knowledge that there was a high probability death would occur.

Ms. Collins said, "Untreated, Amy's death was inevitable." Referring to the day of Amy's death, she stated, "That kid was dead a long time before the EMTs arrived, ladies and gentlemen."

Next to give closing arguments was one of Dr. Shipley's attorneys, Mr. Zahn. He said, "I don't expect you to like it. Nobody would like what you've seen and heard here. But I do expect you to be fair and objective."

Mr. Zahn emphasized that there had been a big appeal to the jurors' emotions. He related that photographs of Amy were often left on display as an attempt to play upon their emotions.

"You saw another photograph where the ribs aren't as prominent and her face isn't as grotesque," he said. "It was a horrible tragedy, but it was not murder."

Dr. Shipley's other attorney, Mr. Voyles, followed his colleague with his closing remarks for the defense. He related that just days before her death, Dr. Shipley had taken Amy to the very places that would have reported child abuse if suspected. He reminded jurors that Dr. Shipley had assisted emergency workers tending to Amy and that it was Dr. Shipley who inserted an intravenous tube into Amy before she was taken to the hospital.

"You have to believe beyond a reasonable doubt that Dr. Shipley knowingly and intentionally killed his daughter. In this courtroom that has not happened," stated Mr. Voyles.

When Deputy Prosecutor Oliver presented her final arguments, she related that Amy fought as much as a five-year-old could before her death, but the Shipleys became her "captors." She said the Shipleys called Danielle a liar.

"They would have you believe she was a mastermind," Ms. Oliver commented. "They call everyone else manipulators."

She also pointed out that the Shipleys had had ten months to sit in jail and consider statements they made to police the day of Amy's death and "plug up the holes." Ms. Oliver asked the jurors not to be swayed by the tears of the couple. "And just because they cry in this courtroom doesn't mean they're not guilty. You don't know who those tears are for," she said.

As Ms. Oliver spoke, I observed the body language of the

three defense attorneys. Mr. Zahn nibbled on his fingernails while Mr. Voyles seemed to hang on every word spoken by her. Gloria's attorney, Mr. Thiros, stared straight ahead.

Mr. Thiros was the last attorney with closing arguments. He noted how no one had corroborated Danielle's stories of ice baths and beatings unless it was to say she had *told* them those stories.

"On cross-examination she wasn't so sure about a lot of things," said Mr. Thiros.

He cited that while the prosecutors questioned Danielle she wiped bangs from her face and on cross-examination she began twirling several stands of longer hair. "It may not mean she was caught in a lie, but it may just be an observation," he stated.

Gloria wept as Mr. Thiros said, "The state tried to paint the ugliest possible picture. Right from the beginning everyone associated with the case was convinced this was murder. Gloria Shipley was not the ugly, wicked stepmother who is now taking over the house. They may be bizarre, but are they criminal? No."

The jury had heard testimony that Dr. Shipley originally told police he had heard Gloria tell Amy to swallow some pepper the night before she died. Later, Dr. Shipley qualified his statement and said he didn't know who issued the instruction. Making a reference to the night before Amy's death, Mr. Thiros said, "Maybe little Danielle had decided to give Amy pepper that night."

All five attorneys had been given the opportunity to give their best shot during the closing arguments. The Shipleys' future was ready to be determined by the jury.

9

The Verdicts (August 21, 1991)

The jury of five men and seven women heard testimony for nine days from twenty-six prosecution witnesses, the Shipleys, and four other defense witnesses. Before the jury adjourned to the jury room, Lake County Superior Court judge Letsinger gave them their instructions. Although the Shipleys had been charged with murder, Judge Letsinger told the jury the couple could be found guilty of involuntary manslaughter or reckless homicide. He said in order for the jury to find the Shipleys guilty of murder, the prosecution must have proven that the Shipleys intended to kill Amy or had known their conduct would result in her death.

"You are the exclusive judges of the evidence, and the decision must be unanimous," Judge Letsinger explained.

The jury deliberated for eight hours before the bailiff announced in front of about thirty spectators awaiting the verdicts that the jury was sequestered for the night. Their attempt to decide the innocence or guilt of Dr. and Mrs. Shipley on charges of child neglect and murder had been unsuccessful on the first day. Deliberations resumed the following morning, and seven hours later they had made their decision.

When the Shipleys were brought from the Lake County jail, which adjoined the court building, Gloria began to cry before the verdicts were read. A gasp of nervous anticipation swept the visitors' area of the packed courtroom as the jurors filed back in with their verdicts. Before the verdicts were read, Judge Letsinger warned the crowd of observers that a contempt-of-court order would be issued if anyone displayed emotion or outbursts.

The judge asked Dr. and Mrs. Shipley, both thirty-five years old, to stand while the verdicts were read by a clerk. The two defendants clung to each other and the only sound heard was Gloria's whimpering as they learned they had been convicted on both charges of murder and child neglect in Amy's death. Dr. Shipley held up his wife as her knees buckled and she started to collapse on two occasions as the guilty verdicts were read.

While Judge Letsinger polled the jurors and all twelve said their verdict was "guilty," Dr. Shipley's head was bowed and his shoulders slumped as Gloria cried uncontrollably. A sentencing date of October 11 was announced by the judge. The Shipleys were then led from the courtroom by bailiffs who permitted their families to grieve privately in a room away from public access.

Outside the courtroom, Ms. Collins and Ms. Oliver hugged each other and were congratulated by fellow deputy prosecutors who had waited with them all day for the verdicts. The jurors had rejected defense arguments that Amy's father, a surgeon, and her stepmother, a former pediatric nurse, did not know their bizarre disciplinary tactics of denying Amy food and force-feeding her pepper would kill the five-year-old child. The verdicts were the harshest the jury could have returned.

"Amy Shipley got justice today," a smiling Ms. Collins told reporters. Ms. Collins said she and Ms. Oliver would ask Judge Letsinger to impose the maximum penalty of sixty years' imprisonment on the Shipleys at their sentencing date. Ms. Collins predicted the verdicts would send a strong message to other abusive parents.

"It's a relief," said Ms. Oliver with tears in her eyes. "The jury made the right decision, but we can't bring her back. Nobody was there for Amy, but maybe another child could be saved with closer attention."

When Ms. Oliver was asked why the Shipleys would have

wanted to starve and abuse their children, she replied, "I wouldn't presume to guess why they did it."

Mr. Zahn said his client's conviction would probably be appealed. Mr. Thiros declined to comment to news reporters.

Jury forewoman Christine Slyser told reporters outside the court building, "It's been stressful on everyone on the jury. It's hard when you have to make a decision about somebody's life."

The other eleven jurors left under police escort without making statements.

When Debbie called me in Vincennes from Crown Point to tell me the jury had found the Shipleys guilty as charged, my first thought was that Danielle and Krista were finally safe. News from Debbie that the system at last had worked certainly lifted my spirits for the future of the two remaining Shipley children.

Debbie returned home and interviewed Vincennes residents who had been most familiar with the abuse Danielle endured. She compiled a story for her newspaper on their reactions to the verdicts.

My principal applauded the jury's decision. Mr. Ritterskamp also said, "However, Amy's death was avoidable. There needs to be more communication and trust between all agencies charged with protecting children. All of us involved will be doing, or have done, a lot of soul-searching to make sure it doesn't occur again."

Vigo Elementary School's nurse, Loretta Perry, commented, "I do hope the little girls will be able to have a stable life."

"They were medical people," remarked Donna Lawrence, the school's attendance officer. "They knew what they were doing. My hope for Danielle is that she can adjust and be able to put this behind her despite the mistreatment."

Jerry McGaughey, the former Knox County prosecutor who had been in charge of the grand jury probe, related that from the facts he read in newspapers, he supported the verdicts from the jury. "The function of the department of welfare was not what it should have been," he said. "I believe if the Welfare Department had proceeded with vigor in Knox County, the whole matter could have been prevented."

Superior Court One judge Edward Theobald said he thought the verdict "was probably deserved.

"I think the authorities in Knox County that dealt with this case handled it properly, according to the information we had at that time," he stated. "They were two intelligent people. What they didn't know at that time, they learned how to manipulate very quickly. We're all very sad about Amy's death."

Part IV
Secrets Revealed

10

The Grand Jury Transcripts
(August 25, 1991)

As anticipated, copies of the transcripts from the 1989 Knox County Grand Jury were sent to the Vincennes *Sun-Commercial* within a few days after the jury's verdict.

·When the paper's attorney was informed of their arrival, Mr. Cummings commented, "This is the first time I can recall grand jury transcripts being released to the public."

Because both conditions in the former court order had been met, the "secrets" were now available for all to know and the "highlights" were summarized in our newspaper. Wanting to know in detail what had happened while the grand jury convened, I could hardly wait to get my hands on those transcripts. When I did, I "burned the midnight oil."

Testimony was heard for two days by area residents who had been selected to serve as grand jurors. An additional grand juror was absent both days. Special Judge Walter Palmer presided, with eight people sworn in for direct examination by the prosecuting attorney, Jerry McGaughey. In order of their appearance, they were Beth Thais, Danielle's caseworker; Donna Lawrence, our school attendance officer; Loretta Perry, Vigo's school nurse; Dr. Ken Buehlman, a Vincennes pediatrician; Dr. Gary Shipley, the alleged perpetrator; Gloria Shipley, Danielle's stepmother; Barbara Morgan, Danielle and Dr. and Mrs. Shipley's counselor; and Judge Edward Theobald of Knox County Superior Court One. I already knew Danielle's name would be missing from the list of those who testified, but I needed to know why. Also, I wanted to find the reasons why Dr. Shipley was not indicted, a question that had been gnawing at me for more than two years.

However, as I read I found myself first drawn to the procedures and protections Danielle deserved for her safety, which appeared questionable to me in the manner they were or were not handled.

During Jerry's opening comments to the grand jury he stated, "Each child abuse case is supposed to be promptly brought before what is called the Child Protection Team. The Child Protection Team is a cross section of the community consisting of about fifteen people who each month meet and hear these types of cases to make a determination as to, well, just to review, I suppose. I'm not sure what the Child Protection Team does do. The statute is vague. To review what the Welfare had done. This case did not come before the Child Protection Team. Sitting on the Child Protection Board is Barbara Morgan, a counselor in this community. At the time I talked to them [Welfare] it had not gone before the Child Protection Team meeting and two months had gone by, at least, from the time the report had been completed. So, two meetings should have occurred. One meeting didn't occur because there was a seminar that the team went to rather than have a meeting."

The Welfare Department had received the report on Danielle's first suspicion of abuse on February 20 and a second alleged abuse on March 17. I was quite disturbed to find out that apparently this Child Protection Team did not have any input into the Shipley case until perhaps May.

In Jerry's remarks providing background information on the case, he described the way his office got Danielle's case report from the Welfare Department and the length of time that elapsed before the prosecutor received it.

He said, "Welfare then made a report to the school saying

they had investigated the matter, and they had. And they wrote down in their own words what occurred. And they checked the blank on the form that is prescribed by the Indiana State Department of Public Welfare that they have to use in these types of cases, showing that the matter was referred to the Prosecutor's Office. Nothing was further heard from the case. Approximately two months went by and the school personnel, the principal, and Patti Bell and people at the school began to talk about why the Prosecutor's Office is doing nothing on the case. My wife happened to work at that particular school. So, she brought the message to me and my reply to her was, 'Well, we have never received anything from Welfare,' and she said, 'Well, that wasn't right because the forms had been laying there since February.' And this is by now June; May, maybe. And that they had seen them in school, that they had been referred to the Prosecutor's Office. So, when I call the head of the Knox County Department of Public Welfare and talk with him, he stated that was incorrect. That no blank had ever been checked showing that it had been referred to the Prosecutor's Office and if it had been checked, it was an error. It shouldn't have been checked, because they had other ways they were going to handle this case."

Jerry explained to the grand jurors that when he obtained the Shipley case report after his call in May to the Welfare Department they had not sent any pictures. He had to call them again, he related, and request the photographs taken by Danielle's caseworker, Beth Thais.

He then stated, "What we found out is that apparently an agreement was reached between the Welfare Department and Dr. Shipley that the matter would be handled if Dr. Shipley and his present wife and Danielle would all seek counseling from the same person, Barbara Morgan."

Jerry added that the Welfare Department then placed Danielle back in Dr. Shipley's physical custody. I reiterate that this return was after only two weeks of foster care.

97

The first individual to speak to the grand jury was Danielle's caseworker. When Mrs. Thais was asked by the prosecutor if she or anybody else had been to Jasper to visit the Shipleys in their home, her reply was: "No." I knew this information from Mrs. Thais's testimony at the trial, and I was still irritated. Danielle was withdrawn from my classroom in late March, and the Shipleys had been living in Jasper for more than three months without a home visit.

During the questioning of Mrs. Morgan about Danielle's referral to her by the Welfare Department, Jerry asked, "Can you recall which specific date?"

"Sure," Mrs. Morgan replied. "I saw her on March 14, when she was brought in by her foster parent. The date of referral was February 21."

"February 21," Jerry repeated.

Mrs. Morgan answered, "Yes."

"She came in March 14?" asked Jerry.

"Yes," she responded.

I remained confused by Mrs. Morgan's answers, because Danielle was not in foster care after March 6. If March 14 was the first time Mrs. Morgan saw her, as recorded in the transcripts, Danielle did not receive any therapy while she was in her foster care.

As Mrs. Morgan's testimony continued, she stated, "Danielle apparently, it's my understanding, that the school, Vigo Elementary, called the Welfare Department because Danielle came to school with her multiple bruises. The bruises were on her thighs and on her hands and some on her face, I believe. By the time I saw her the bruises were gone, so I have only seen pictures of them."

I was not confused with the facts that Mrs. Morgan did not get a firsthand observation of the physical pain Danielle had been dealt by her father and that therapy had not been provided while Danielle's physical signs of abuse were healing.

There were frequent discussions and opinions about whether Danielle should or should not testify.

In Jerry's opening remarks to the grand jury he told them, "The Welfare Department then came in yesterday and filed a motion to quash the subpoena for the child. So, the child cannot come before you and testify to you. For some reason, they want to withhold from you what the child has to say. The grounds for their motion to quash is that they think it would be detrimental to the child's well-being to have to testify."

He then pointed out that even though equipment for videotaping was in the basement of the courthouse, the Welfare Department had never videotaped any statements from Danielle.

Later in his opening statements, the prosecutor again spoke to the Welfare Department's motion to quash Danielle's subpoena. Jerry explained, "The judge has not ruled on the motion to quash. He called me yesterday when he received it and asked what I thought about it. I said I thought it was important that a child in a child abuse case come in and testify."

When Dr. Shipley testified, he portrayed Danielle as a most difficult little girl with numerous problems. He cited examples of her being totally out of control and depicted her as being unreliable. Gloria Shipley reinforced her husband's prior testimony presenting a severe-problem-child image of Danielle. Dr. Shipley's statements about his daughter, supported by his wife, and his knack for making people feel sorry for him could have had an influence on why Danielle did not appear in front of the grand jury and why he was not brought to trial.

On the second and final day Jerry addressed the grand jury, telling them it would appear, after sifting through evidence from the previous day, Danielle didn't need to be called as a witness. He said, "Gary Shipley has come in to this grand jury after having been given his constitutional warnings, has admitted that he has stricken his child, Danielle. That resulted in the bruises that we saw. I suppose that is really the issue here. So I think the elements

99

of certain crimes are already before the grand jury."

Jerry asked if the grand jurors were ready for deliberations. The foreman, Roy Hunter, reported they were not. It was requested they talk to Barbara Morgan, Rhonda Shipley, and Judge Theobald before they made a decision. Jerry informed them he could not get Rhonda Shipley on that day, but Mrs. Morgan and Judge Theobald were called.

A member of the grand jury, Connie Reitmeyer, asked Mrs. Morgan a question: "In your past experiences with counseling, do you feel like this can be a normal family?"

Mrs. Morgan responded, "I feel if Gary and Gloria are willing to continue and keep making progress that I have seen in the last month that, yes, this family can at least be normal. I do see them working a lot harder than initially. I see them a little more willing to look at some things than they were initially. In all fairness, that's not atypical. In working with abused children and the perpetrators or the people that abused them, denial is a very normal part of that process. I feel that we are finally beyond the point of denial. You know, when looking at the alternative of treatment versus prosecution, I feel that if Dr. Shipley went through the prosecution process, there would never be a chance for this child. Well, I won't say never. The chance for this child to work through this would be ten times as difficult. Because children have a tendency when they are physically abused, they have two choices: they can say, 'It is all my fault,' or 'It is my parents' fault.' Children believe their parents are gods. They must in order to survive. Young children have to have all of the dependency needs met by their parents. If they believe that their parents are bad, then they have nobody to meet their needs and then they are lost. So then what children do is what Danielle has done, and that is, they blame themselves. 'I must be getting hit, I must be getting in trouble, because somehow I am bad.' And then, if she has to go through that process of testifying in court, being the one to come in front of people and in front of her parents and say, 'My parents did this;

my father did this to me,' and he ends up, for instance, going to jail, then what happens is she feels that it is her fault. And then she has to live with that guilt for the rest of her life. You know, there are times when I feel prosecution is, well, is the best alternative. That's when a child cannot be protected from this person. That's when the person isn't willing to admit what has happened, isn't willing to work on change. And the most important [thing] is that the child can't ever be safe. I don't think that's the case in this family. If Gary and Gloria continue working as they have over the last month, I feel Danielle's chances of healing and growing from here on are better if she can stay in the family and work with the family to heal some of these scars that have been inflicted on her in her first five years of her life."

Judge Theobald informed the grand jury that Danielle, Gloria, and Dr. Shipley were required through his court to continue counseling. This psychological help would be monitored and reviewed every six months.

Jerry inquired, "The dispositional plan, over what period of time will that occur?"

"It will continue until the court decides that the matter has been resolved," Judge Theobald answered.

"So it is indeterminate now?" Jerry asked.

Judge Theobald responded, "It is indeterminate, that is correct."

Jerry asked again, "So it could last for a year or several years?"

"It could last for two or three years, could last until she is eighteen," the judge said.

At the first court review, six months later, wardship of Danielle was returned to Dr. Shipley with the Welfare Department asking it be continued with them. Judge Theobald had said when he made the decision that Dr. Shipley had complied with all the court had asked of him.

The last question the prosecutor asked Judge Theobald was:

"In your opinion, would anything be accomplished, either positively or negatively, by criminal prosecuting of Gary Shipley for child abuse in this case?"

Judge Theobald replied, "I do have an opinion on that, and it is my opinion that it would be more harmful to Danielle to have to not only appear before this body to testify once, but she would then again have to testify before the court, probably in this courtroom, and I think that if there was a trial and an indictment returned we would be revictimizing the victim, making her a victim again. I don't think that anything really can, anything more can, be accomplished. If her father were sent to prison, that would be an extremely traumatic experience, I think, for her. She would feel that she was at fault for sending him away, and I don't know that she could ever recover from that."

The final two witnesses, Mrs. Morgan and Judge Theobald, had given testimony showing the Welfare Department was not alone in wanting to stop Danielle from testifying. They also provided testimony against the prosecution of Dr. Shipley. There was no reference to the judge's decision on the motion to quash Danielle's subpoena. Regardless, the victim did not testify.

There were conflicting reasons for Danielle's hair loss offered by the people subpoenaed. They were that Danielle's hair had been pulled out by her father or both parents or she had lost it due to a medical disease or a physical reaction to the stress she was undergoing. Dr. Bruce Mallatt's name was given by the Shipleys in Loretta's testimony as the Vincennes dermatologist who treated Danielle for her medical problems.

After hearing Mrs. Thais, Donna, and Loretta, the grand juror Mrs. Reitmeyer asked Jerry, "How about Dr. Mallatt? Is he going to come in?"

Jerry replied, "No, he hasn't been subpoenaed, but it would probably be a good idea to subpoena him."

The proceedings continued with Dr. Buehlman, Dr. Shipley, and Mrs. Morgan responding to the issue of Danielle's loss of hair when asked. Dr. Mallatt did not come before the grand jury.

Missing from the transcripts was Vigo Elementary School's second report, a transcript of a phone call from Mr. Ritterskamp to the Welfare Department on March 17 about Danielle having been forced by her father to drink liquid shampoo. As Danielle's caseworker, Mrs. Thais should have known this, since the Welfare Department had been informed. Mrs. Morgan was told about Danielle saying she had to drink shampoo in late March by our school social worker. Both testified, but this incident of abuse was not mentioned by either party to the grand jury.

As I explained in an earlier chapter, I did not know the grand jury was going to discuss the Shipleys before I left Indiana to go on my vacation. It was logical to me that my principal would have been subpoenaed when it became known I was unable to respond to my subpoena. He had twice reported Danielle's alleged abuse to the Welfare Department. He had access to my documentations, which were in the school safe. But Mr. Ritterskamp was not subpoenaed.

Nothing was discussed in the transcripts about Dr. Shipley having been investigated by the DEA while he lived in Vincennes. This rumor had circulated around our town on more than one occasion before the grand jury was assembled. According to the transcripts, hearsay could be considered by the grand jury.

Because of their profession, perhaps Dr. Daniel Neumann or Dr. Jay Tuttle, the two surgeons with whom Dr. Shipley practiced medicine before he moved to Jasper, might have heard about Dr. Shipley's problem with the DEA. Possibly they could have shed some light on this situation if they had been subpoenaed. Of course, nobody could have been asked if the Prosecutor's Office was unaware of the investigation. The fact remained that there was no reference to this investigation of Dr. Shipley in front of the grand jury.

Before the grand jury was gathered to examine Danielle's alleged abuse, Vigo Elementary School personnel and I were convinced there were enough facts to prosecute Dr. Shipley. After analyzing the 263 pages of transcripts, I believe a primary reason the case was dismissed was because there was relevant information the grand jury did not receive. Other significant factors were the reassurances and recommendations by reputable professionals in our community.

I have second-guessed the grand jury with the advantage of hindsight to criticize their decision. The fact remains that the decision not to indict Dr. Shipley had to be based on the testimony of those individuals who appeared before the grand jury.

Part V
Payment for the Crime

11

The Sentencing (October 11, 1991)

Because I had made a personal decision several months ago to follow the Shipley case until it was finalized in our court system, I requested a personal day to attend the sentencing of Dr. and Mrs. Shipley on October 11, 1991. Naturally, Debbie went to cover the story, and we were joined by Mike Cady, the news director of WZDM 92.1 FM radio. The three of us drove to Crown Point after work the day before the sentencing hearing to stay all night in order to be in the courtroom early the next morning.

In our motel room, we expressed joy over the fact that this would be our last trip involving the Shipley couple. We rehashed the case, talking about the trial's vivid and troubling images which continued to haunt us.

Debbie commented, "Can you ever forget those graphic photographs of Amy's body taken during her autopsy? I can still see those bruises on most of her frail body, her bones prominently showing under her skin, and her dried and cracked lips. Many times at night as I try to go to sleep, I picture Amy's recessed eyes fixed right at me."

"I am having a great deal of trouble with the same things you are," I answered. "I can only imagine the pain Amy endured the months before her death."

"She must have been terrified night after night, forced to sleep on what appeared to be a cold bathroom floor," said Debbie.

"My kindergartners are counting the days until Halloween,"

I stated. "I need to join in their anticipation, but Halloween will never be quite the same for me because of Amy's final Halloween. Gary and Gloria spoiled the holiday for me when Danielle told how they had Amy watch Krista and her put on their costumes, go trick-or-treating, and eat their candy when she was not allowed to join them in any of these childhood pleasures."

Debbie related, "I'll never feel the same about pepper either. Every time I use pepper, I think of Amy." Then Debbie asked, "Who ever heard of 'stealing food'? When I was growing up, my parents would never have considered eating a cookie 'stealing food.' If it wasn't close to mealtime, my brother and I always had food available to us whenever we were hungry. Isn't that the way it is supposed to be?"

"Of course!" I replied.

"How do you feel about tomorrow?" Debbie inquired.

I answered, "Stewing about the sentencing is useless." As I turned off the light, I remarked, "Judge Letsinger has earned our respect. I truly am convinced he will make the correct evaluations of this hideous case."

The following morning we met Mike and arrived at the courtroom in ample time. When Judge Letsinger called the sentencing hearing to order, the attorneys made their final attempts to influence the length of the sentence to be imposed. Both deputy prosecutors asked the judge for the Shipleys to receive the maximum sentence, contending they had violated their responsibilities as parents and as professionals.

Ms. Oliver said, "Gloria Shipley's claims of loving the children were little more than 'window dressing.'" Ms. Oliver described the treatment of Amy as torture and a heinous crime.

"The crime was one that 'shakes me to the core' and portrayed the 'darker side' of human character," stated Ms. Collins.

Attorneys for the Shipleys asked that the sentences for the charges run concurrently because they stemmed from the same act.

Mr. Thiros stated that the Shipley trial attracted more attention than any other case he could recall in his thirty-three years of practice in Lake County, his client had been portrayed as the evil stepmother by the media, and Gloria Shipley was only a parent trying to cope with Amy's behavior problems. Mr. Thiros asked Judge Letsinger to consider a letter Rhonda Shipley had written concerning the judge's decision.

"Although she is bitter and hurt, she realizes that sooner or later Danielle and Krista are going to have to face their father and Gloria," Mr. Thiros said. "Rhonda wanted this meeting to take place somewhere outside prison and while there is enough life in Gary."

The lawyer further explained that Rhonda wanted the judge to take this into consideration and also wanted the couple incarcerated until the children were adults.

Mr. Thiros said, "Rhonda also suggested the judge sentence the couple to a term that upon their release they be able to salvage something of their lives, if they so choose."

Judge Letsinger said he had had sleepless nights thinking about the case.

"That photo of Amy keeps coming back to me," the judge stated. He related, "I keep seeing Dr. Shipley using a pointer and clinically going over the photograph, pointing out this and that point."

Judge Letsinger said he did not see the Shipleys showing any remorse for their actions. He did say he saw remorse when the verdict was read.

"I saw remorse over the situation you're in," said the judge as he sternly looked at the Shipleys.

Judge Letsinger noted the victim's age, the fact that the Shipleys had ignored advice from experts on dealing with family problems, and how they had moved around to avoid possible detection of the family's continuing problems.

Gloria dabbed at her eyes periodically during the hearing

while Dr. Shipley sat emotionless. When Judge Letsinger asked if they had anything to say, Gloria told him she didn't do anything that she believed would cause harm to Amy. Dr. Shipley did not utter a sound.

Then, Judge Letsinger sentenced each to fifty years on the murder charge and fifteen years on the charge of neglect. Even though I knew the Shipleys would be given credit for their time already served, which was 338 days, and they could be eligible for parole in half the sentenced time for good behavior under Indiana law, I was content, at last, with the sixty-five-year sentence. Debbie and I exchanged a quick look of satisfaction, not daring to whisper a word to each other until court was adjourned.

As soon as we left the courtroom, Debbie, Mike, and I joined Ms. Collins, Ms. Oliver, and Detective Ed Davies for lunch. The two Lake County deputy prosecutors had almost a year to think about the circumstances surrounding the Shipley case, and they reflected on them.

"Initially, Dr. Shipley and Gloria had enough smarts to somewhat fool the system and acted like they would comply," Ms. Oliver said. "They gave enough background for a problem with Danielle to try to put out the impression they were just mistaken people, much like they argued at the trial."

Ms. Oliver stated, "With what the Vincennes community had to work with, those involved probably thought they were doing the right thing. In hindsight, it's not the right thing. Certainly a little more supervision would have been better. Had they not been a doctor and a nurse they would not have been given as much credibility as perhaps the average person."

She also explained, "Maybe on the face of things, the Shipleys were cooperative. So, I think they were handled perhaps as well as they should have been, but you can't really finger-point at any specific thing and say, 'This should be different,' without the information we have now."

Ms. Oliver added, "I think, too, it goes to human nature, in the sense that you don't want to believe that a parent is capable of doing this to a child. In this case it was once again compounded by the fact Gary was a doctor and Gloria was a nurse.

"The one problem regarding the system, and it's well intended, is the eventual goal to reunite the family," remarked Ms. Oliver, who was once employed as a caseworker by a Welfare Department. "As long as you have that, you have to give families the opportunity to comply. And knowing how important it is to have a child grow up with their own parents, whenever it is possible, in that respect you have to work within the system."

Ms. Oliver said, "There is a wide spectrum of cases coming through the court system that deal with physical abuse. Perhaps those cases, which I consider serious, should be treated differently than ones that involve dirty living conditions or something similar. So you can take a harder look, when you're a welfare worker, at those cases than you would at other cases.

"Once a report has been made to a Welfare Department," commented Ms. Oliver, "I do not believe a caseworker can determine if a child is being abused with three or four 'announced' home visits. I certainly think you should have 'unannounced' visits as often as possible and other checks and balances within the family itself. Maybe relatives or somebody else can check to see if this kid is being bruised."

Ms. Oliver stated, "I believe a child should be in therapy before the decision is made to place the child back into an allegedly abusive home. Also, I believe a child should be in separate therapy from the parents. The child is not going to be free to face the abuser and say what is happening in the home. You certainly cannot take what the parents are saying at face value."

Ms. Collins explained, "The Shipley case was exceptional based on the fact of the educational attainment of both the defendants and assurances they made to bring their conduct within what people recognize as acceptable. Through their knowledge and intelligence, the Shipleys were able to 'pull the right strings' and give the answers people wanted to hear. By telling everyone they would comply with laws and guidelines, they were able to get through the system without too much trouble. I am unsure an 'average' person would be capable of manipulating the system as did the Shipleys."

"Another bottom-line problem is that people just aren't willing enough to believe children," Ms. Oliver stated. "It's so easy to rationalize what a child has to say because they are not capable of expressing themselves like an adult. Until more people are more willing to pay attention to them and realize kids don't always make up stories about things to get their parents in trouble, things won't change."

Epilogue: 1995

Today Danielle and Krista Shipley live with their mother, Rhonda, in Indianapolis. Danielle and I correspond at Christmas and on her birthday. Rhonda sends me both girls' school pictures with updates on their active participation in school and church activities.

Since I have met Hope and Bob Hanlon, Rhonda's parents, we have become friends. As Rhonda, Danielle, and Krista rebuild their lives together, Hope and Bob contribute in a supporting role, as they are once again functioning as a family.

Dr. Gary Shipley died on June 24, 1992, after he suffered a severe relapse of asthma in the Indiana Reformatory at Pendleton. A spokesman for the Indiana Department of Correction said Dr. Shipley had had the illness since before he was sentenced eight months earlier to sixty-five years in prison and was being treated for his asthma in prison. He was thirty-six years old at the time of his death.

In August of 1993, the Indiana Court of Appeals reviewed six issues raised by the appeal of Gloria Shipley:

1. *Whether there was a double-jeopardy violation when the trial court imposed consecutive sentences of murder and neglect of a dependent.* The court of Appeals overturned Gloria's neglect of a dependent conviction and fifteen-year sentence, deciding both charges were based on the same acts during the same period of time. The ruling read: "Because the pattern of neglect was the means by which the

murder was committed, double jeopardy precluded her conviction and sentencing for both offenses." Therefore, Gloria's total sentence of sixty-five years was reduced by fifteen years. The appeals court upheld Gloria's murder conviction and fifty-year sentence by supporting the trial court in the remaining five issues of Gloria's appeal.

2. *Whether the trial court erred in failing to grant a mistrial when the Lake County jury was briefly exposed to suppressed evidence during its deliberation.* The jury had been deliberating for less than one half hour when a portion of Dr. Shipley's voluntary statement to the police was discovered. The statements were removed by the bailiff. The opinion from the court was that the questions concerned Gary Shipley, not Gloria.

3. *Whether there was a break in the chain of custody of blood samples taken from Amy.* The defense wanted jurors to believe that Amy's blood samples were mishandled and therefore the drug in her blood could have gotten there after her death.

4. *Whether the trial court committed an error by allowing the prosecutors to question the Shipleys concerning Gloria's sexual preference for Gary Shipley's first wife and his medical license restriction.* The defense tried to object to the line of questioning of Rhonda and Gloria's relationship because they felt it was irrelevant to the case. The same applied to Dr. Shipley's medical license restriction.

5. *Whether the trial court erred in not inquiring further into an allegation of a coerced verdict.* Gloria contended that one juror was forced into saying the defendants were guilty. The trial court polled each juror after the guilty verdicts were read. All the jurors answered in the affirmative, demonstrating the jury's verdicts were unanimous. The jury deliberated for about one and a half days before reaching a verdict.

6. *Whether there was sufficient evidence to sustain her murder conviction.* The defense believed the prosecution had not presented enough evidence to support a murder conviction.

Gloria Shipley is serving her fifty-year sentence at the Indiana Women's Prison in Indianapolis.